LACON

OR

MANY THINGS IN FEW WORDS;

ADDRESSED TO
THOSE WHO THINK

BY THE REV. C. C. COLTON

(Published in London, 1826)

Edited
By
George J. Barbour

Published by

MELROSE BOOKS

An Imprint of Melrose Press
St Thomas Place, Ely
Cambridgeshire
CB7 4GG
www.melrosebooks.com

FIRST EDITION

This Arrangement and Editing
Copyright © George J. Barbour 2001

Cover designed by Geoff Hobbs Design

ISBN 0 9548480 5 5

Printed and bound in Great Britain by:
Bath Press Limited, Lower Bristol Road,
Bath, BA2 3BL, UK

Dedication

This book is for Anita with love.

Acknowledgement

I would like to express my sincere thanks to Alan Barbour, Don Day and Ann Merideth, whose continuing interest and professional editorial comments have contributed greatly to the completion of this book.

I thank Michael Williamson of Brisbane, Australia for his interest in *Lacon* and his contributions to Reverend Colton's family history. Williamson is a great, great, great grand nephew of Reverend Colton.

From 1821 to 2001 — (Editor's Note)

This book *"Lacon, or Many Things in few Words"* was first published in 1821. It has lain, apparently unnoticed and uncared for, for over one hundred and eighty years. It is a good book; I think it is a great book, and I feel fortunate to play some small part in its resurrection.

In the winter of 1974-1975, my wife, Anita and I went to live in Oxford, UK, for what amounted to a private sabbatical for six months. We were both compulsive readers and we thought Oxford would be the place to go to read. One day I was rummaging around in the used book shelves of Blackwell's, perhaps the best book store in the world, and I bought a copy of *"Lacon"*. I had never heard of the book or its author, but it looked like a collection of interesting ideas, so I bought it for a couple of pounds. Later the same day, I stopped in at the Bodleian Library and retrieved some material on Charles Caleb Colton and had it photocopied. When we went home in the spring, the book and the biographical material went with us. I put it on a shelf of our modest library, and I never looked at it again for the next twenty-five years.

Last year, looking for something to do I opened my copy of *"Lacon"* for the first time. As a result; for the past several months, I have occupied myself with the writings of that very remarkable man, Reverend Charles Caleb Colton. I have enjoyed choosing among hundreds of wide-ranging ideas; selecting those that seemed the most entertaining. To make the selection of material easier, I have added descriptive captions to the original material and arranged them in alphabetical order by subject. It is my earnest hope that any reader, who may happen upon this book, will have as much pleasure reading it as I have had in rearranging it.

G. J. B.

Introducing Reverend Charles Caleb Colton

"COLTON, Charles Caleb (c.1780-1832) clergyman, sportsman, gambler, suicide, and author of the aphoristic *Lacon* (2 vol. 1820-1822)"
Chambers Biographical Dictionary, Edinburgh, W. R. Chambers, 1914

Reverend Charles Caleb Colton was a man of great intellect and energy. He had a prodigious appetite for knowledge and a driving need to share it. In his 52 years of life, he produced a substantial body of writing; both prose and poetry, which for elegance, grace and wit could hardly be equaled; certainly not by many present-day writers. After almost 200 years, his mordant comments — on doctors, generals, lawyers, priests, politicians and other characters have a contemporary flavour and sting that provide rewards for the brighter than average reader.

Colton's "*Lacon*", written during the years 1820 and 1821 and published in London in 1821, is a two-volume work containing some 800 aphorisms, numerous essays of varying lengths and a poem of epic length; all of which are tributes to the author's talent, energy and range of interests.

The best way to become acquainted with an author is to sample his writings, particularly those in which he reveals his personal viewpoints on the business of writing; the pleasures and pitfalls of that trade and his sure and abiding belief that writing is the only civilized way for a gentleman to make a living.
What follows is a selection of excerpts from Colton's remarks in two prefaces to the two volumes of "*Lacon*". In addition to these, I have included some comments on related topics which he included in his collection of aphorisms.

G. J. Barbour, Editor

*   *   *

"He that studies books alone, will know how things ought to be; and he that studies men will know how things are; and it would have been impossible to have written these pages, without mixing somewhat more freely with the world, than inclination might prompt, or judgment approve. For observations made in the cloister, or in the desert, will generally be as obscure as the one, and as barren as the other; but he that would paint with his pen, no less than he that would paint with his pencil, must study originals, and not be over fearful of a little dust."

*   *   *

"Justice to my readers compels me to admit that I write because I have nothing to do, justice to myself induces me to add, that I will cease to write the moment *I have nothing to say*. Discretion has been termed the better part of valour, and it is more certain, that diffidence is the better part of knowledge. Where I am ignorant, and know that I am so, I am silent."

*   *   *

"There are two classes of people that profit little by reading, those that are very wise, and those that are very foolish. I cannot presume to inform the one, and I cannot hope to improve the other. I have therefore attempted to make "*Lacon*" an intelligible book, capable of doing some good to that valuable class of the community who have *other* things to do as well as to read, and who when they snatch a few hours from their occupations, to devote to literary pursuits, must necessarily prefer that author who gives them the most knowledge, and takes from them the least time."

*　　　*　　　*

"The great error of our authors is that they sit down to *make* a book rather than to write. To combine profundity with perspicuity, wit with judgment, solidity with vivacity, truth with novelty, and *all* of them with liberality, who is sufficient for these things? — a very serious question. But it is one which authors had much better propose to themselves *before* publication, than have it proposed to them, by their editors after it."

*　　　*　　　*

"I have addressed this volume to *those who think*, and some may accuse me of an ostentatious independence, in presuming to inscribe a book to so small a minority. But a volume addressed to those *who think* is in fact addressed to all the world, for although the proportion of those who *do* think, be extremely small, yet every individual flatters himself that he is *one* of that number."

*　　　*　　　*

"In fact, every author is a far better judge of the pains that his efforts have cost him, than any reader could possibly be; but to *what* purpose he has taken those pains, this is a question on which his readers will not allow the author a voice, nor even an opinion; from the tribunal of the public there is no appeal, and it is fit that it should be so, otherwise we should not only have rivers of ink expended in bad writing, but oceans more in defending it; for he that writes in a bad style, is sure to *retort* in a worse."

*　　　*　　　*

"On subjects on which mankind have been thinking for so many thousands of years, it will often happen that whatever is absolutely new, may have the misfortune to be absolutely false. It is a melancholy consideration for authors, that there is very little "*Terrra Incognita*" in literature, and there remain to us moderns, only two roads to success: discovery and conquest. If indeed we can advance any propositions that are both *true* and *new*, these are indisputably our own, by right of discovery; and if we can repeat what is old, more briefly and brightly than others, this also becomes ours, by right of conquest."

*　　　*　　　*

"With respect to the style, I have adopted in the following sheets, I have attempted to make it vary with the subject; avoiding all pomp of words, where there was no corresponding elevation of ideas; for such turgidity although it be aspiring as that of the balloon is also as useless. I have neither spare time for superfluous printing, nor spare money for superfluous printing, and shall be satisfied, if I have not missed of brightness, in pursuit of brevity."

*   *   *

"It has cost me more time and pains to *abridge* these pages than to write them. Perhaps that is nearly the perfection of good writing, which *is* original, but whose truth alone prevents the reader from suspecting that it is so: and which affects that for knowledge, which the lens affects for the sun-beam, when it condenses its brightness, in order to increase its force."

*   *   *

"How far the following efforts will stand the test of this criterion, is not for me to determine; to know is one thing, to do is another, and it may be observed of good writing, as of good blood, that it is much easier to say what it is composed of, than to compose it."

*   *   *

"But above all, I do most earnestly hope, that none will accuse me of usurping, on this occasion, the chair of the moralist, or of presuming to deliver any thing here advanced, as oracular, magisterial, dictatorial or 'ex cathedra'. I have no opinions that I would not most willingly exchange for truth. I may be sometimes wrong, I may be sometimes right; at all events discussion may be provoked, and as this cannot be done without thought, even that is a good."

*   *   *

"I despise dogmatism in others, too much to indulge in it myself; I have not been led to these opinions by the authority of great names; for I have always considered rather *what* is said, than *who* said it; and the consequence of their argument; rather than the consequence of him who delivers it. It is sufficiently humiliating to our nature, to reflect that our knowledge is but as the rivulet, our ignorance as the sea."

*   *   *

"I have said that the maxims in the following pages are written upon this principle — *that men are the same;* upon this alone it is that the sacred maxim which forms the golden hinge of our religion, rests and revolves, '*Do unto thy neighbour as thou would that he should do unto thee*'. The proverbs of Solomon suit all places and all times, because Solomon knew mankind, and mankind are ever the same. No revolution has taken place in the body, nor in the mind. Four thousand years ago, men shivered with frost, and panted with heat, were *cold* in their gratitude, and *ardent* in their revenge — Should my readers think some of my conclusions are too severe,

13

they will in justice recollect, that my object is truth, that my subject *is man* and that a handsome picture cannot represent deformity."

*   *   *

"There are three difficulties in authorship: to write any thing worth the publishing, to find honest men to publish it, and to get sensible men to read it."

*   *   *

"I wish to make some observations on anecdotes, and I think I may as well take this opportunity as another. Imprimis, I am not so particular about their originality, as their application. If an anecdote comes across my mind, which tends to the support of any argument or proposition, I hesitate not to adduce it. There are no anecdotes in these pages that will be new to all my readers, and perhaps there are none but may be new to some of them. Those to whom any anecdote is old, will not be offended, and if it be well applied; and those to whom it may be new, will receive the double pleasure of novelty and of illustration."

"In fact, there are only two modes by which an anecdote can be perfectly original; the parties, who relate it, must either have heard it *from* or made it *for* the principals. Anecdotes, like the air, are private property, only so long as they are kept in; the instant the one is told, or the other is liberated, they are common stock."

"But the principal reason that has induced me to intersperse these pages with anecdotes, is to tempt young minds to a higher and more intellectual kind of reading — I have occasionally attempted to lead on young minds by anecdotes; they will in all probability be new to them, and I have endeavoured so to write them, that he that runs may read, and he that reads, may understand."

*   *   *

"Many books require no thought from those who read them and for a very simple reason — they make no such demand upon those who wrote them. Those works therefore are the most valuable, that set our thinking faculties in the fullest operation. For as the solar light calls forth all the latent powers, and the dormant principles of vegetation contained in the kernel, but which, without such a stimulus, would neither have struck roots downward, nor borne fruit upwards, so it is with the light that is intellectual; it calls forth and awakens into energy those latent principles of thought in the minds of others, which without this stimulus, reflection would not have matured, or examination improved, nor action embodied."

*   *   *

"With books as with companions, it is of more consequence to know which to avoid, than which to choose; for good books are as scarce as good companions; and in both instances, all that we can learn from bad ones, is that so much time has been worse than thrown away. That writer does the most that gives his reader the *most* knowledge, and takes from him the *least* time — I do not pretend to have attained this, I have only attempted it. One thing I may affirm, that I have first considered whether it be worth while to say a thing *at all*, before I have taken any trouble to say it well, knowing that words are but air and that both are capable of much *condensation*. Words indeed are but the signs and *counters* of knowledge, and their currency should be strictly regulated by the *capital* they represent."

*   *   *

"In the preface to the first volume of *Lacon*, I have observed that there are but two modes to obtain celebrity in authorship; discovery, or conquest. Discovery, by saying what none others have said, with this proviso, that it be true as well as new, and conquest, by saying what others have said, but with more point, brevity and brightness. To demand that any writer, be his powers or *caliber* what they may, should avail himself of no materials whatever, except those that arise out of his own resources and invention, is as unjust and extravagant as it would be to insist that a Michael Angelo or a Canova, should have no credit for a statue, because they did not create the block of marble from which it was produced.

Readers of taste and candor will perceive the drift of this article, and apply it. If not according to my hopes, assuredly, according to my deserts. I am certain it is a very easy thing to find fault with a work embracing so many topics as this which I have attempted, and I am as certain that it would find one. To those who shall accomplish this to be a very useful thing to produce something similar but superior, I shall freely forgive the other."

*   *   *

"Criticism is like champagne, nothing more execrable if bad, nothing more excellent if good; if meager, muddy, vapid and sour, both are fit only to engender colic and wind. But if rich, generous and sparkling, they communicate a genial glow to the spirits, improve the taste, expand the heart, and are worthy of being introduced at the symposium of the Gods."

"In the whole range of literature, nothing is more entertaining, and I might add, more instructive than sound and legitimate criticism, the disinterested convictions of a man of sensibility. Who enters rather into the spirit, than the letter of his author, who can follow him to the height of his compass, and, while he sympathizes with every brilliant power, and genuine passion of the poet, is not so far carried out of himself, as to indulge his admiration at the expense of his judgment, but who can afford us the double pleasure of being first pleased with his author, and secondly with himself, for having given us such just and incontrovertible reasons for our approbation."

*   *   *

"Modern criticism discloses that which it would fain conceal, but conceals that which it professes to disclose; it is, therefore, read by the discerning, not to discover the merits of an author, but the motives of his critic."

15

Index

Aphorisms

*Entries marked with a * indicate a comment with that entry*

Adversity as Teacher
He that has never known adversity is but half acquainted with others, or with himself. Constant success shows us but one side of the world. For, as it surrounds us with friends, who will tell us only our merits, so it silences those enemies from whom alone we can learn our defects.

Adversity vs. Prosperity
He that has never suffered extreme adversity knows not the full extent of his own deprivation, and he that has never enjoyed the summit of prosperity, is equally ignorant how far the iniquity of *others* can go. For our adversity will excite temptations in ourselves, our prosperity in *others.* Sir Robert Walpole observed it was fortunate that few men could be prime ministers, because it was fortunate that few men could know the profligacy of the human mind. Therefore a beautiful woman, if poor, should use a double circumspection: for her beauty will tempt *others,* her poverty *herself.*

Advice; thrusting it on others
When we feel a strong desire to thrust our advice upon others, it is usually because we suspect their weakness, but we ought rather to suspect our own.

Advice or Approbation
We ask advice, but we mean approbation.

Advice to the Old: be cheerful
The young fancy that their follies are mistaken by the old for happiness, and the old fancy that their gravity is mistaken by the young, for wisdom. And yet each is wrong in supposing this of the other. The misapprehension is mutual, but I shall not attempt to set either of them right, because their respective error is reciprocally consolatory to both. I would not be so severe, as the lively Frenchman, who said, that if they were fond of giving advice, it was only because they were no longer able to set a bad example; but for their own sake, no less than of others, I would recommend cheerfulness to the old, in the room of austerity, knowing that *heaviness* is much more synonymous with ignorance than *gravity* with wisdom. Cheerfulness ought to be the *viaticum vitae** of their life to the old; age without cheerfulness is a Lapland winter without a sun; and this spirit of cheerfulness should be encouraged in our youth, if we would wish to have the benefit of it in our old age; time will make a generous wine more mellow; but it will turn that which is *early on the fret,*** to vinegar.
* provisions for the journey of life
**secondary fermentation

Affection; want of, effects
There are some who affect a want of affectation, and flatter themselves that they are above flattery; they are proud of being thought extremely humble, and would go round the world to punish those who thought them capable of revenge; they are so satisfied of the suavity of their own temper, that they would quarrel with their dearest benefactor only for doubting it. And yet so very blind are all their acquaintances to

these their numerous qualifications and merits, that the possessor of them invariably discovers, when it is too late, that they have lived in the world without a single friend, and are about to leave it, without a single mourner.

Age and Love

Age and love associate not, if they are ever allied, the firmer the friendship, the more fatal its termination, and an old man, like a spider* can never make love, without beating his own death watch.

* It may not be generally known that the male spider is supplied with a little bladder somewhat similar to a drum. The ticking noise which has been termed the death watch, is nothing more than the sound he makes upon this little apparatus, in order to serenade and to allure *his mistress.*

Ambition; the dangers of

Ambition is to the mind, what the cap is to the falcon; it *blinds* us first, and then compels us to tower, by reason of our blindness. But alas, when we are at the summit of a vain ambition, we are at the depth of real misery. We are placed where time cannot improve, but must impair us; in short, by attaining all we wish, and gaining all we want, we have only reached a pinnacle, where we have nothing to hope, but everything to fear.

Anger; defence of

The intoxication of anger, like that of the grape, shows us to others, but hides us from ourselves; and we injure our own cause, in the opinion of the world, when we too passionately and eagerly defend it; like the father of Virginia, who murdered his daughter to prevent her violation. Neither will all men be disposed to view our quarrels precisely in the same light that we do; and a man's blindness to his own defects, will ever increase, in proportion as he is angry with others, or pleased with himself.

Anger and Revenge

The sun should not set upon our anger; neither should he rise upon our confidence. We should forgive freely, but forget rarely. I will not be revenged, and this I owe to my enemy; but I will remember, and this I owe to myself.

Anguish of Mind or Body

Anguish of mind has driven thousands to suicide; anguish of body, none. This proves that the healthiness of mind is of far more consequence to our happiness than the health of the body, although both are deserving of much more attention than either of them receive.

Antiquarian; he remembers and forgets

A thorough paced antiquarian not only remembers what all other people have thought proper to forget, but he also forgets what all other people think is proper to remember.

Antiquities; looking back
To look back to antiquity is one thing, to go back to it is another; if we go backwards to antiquity, it should be as those that are winning a race; to press forwards the faster, and to leave the beaten till farther behind.

Applause; the spur of noble minds
Applause is the spur of noble minds, the end and aim of weak ones.

Arbitration; advantage of
Arbitration has this advantage; there are some points of contest which it is better to *lose* by arbitration, than to win by law. But as a good general offers his terms before the action, rather than in the midst of it, so a wise man will not easily be persuaded to have recourse to a reference, when once his opponent has dragged him into a court.

Arts of Destruction and Preservation
The art of destruction seems to have proceeded geometrically, while the art of preservation cannot be said to have advanced even in a plain arithmetical progression; for there are but *two* specifics known, which will infallibly cure their two respective diseases. But the modes of destroying life have increased so rapidly, that conquerors have not to consider how to murder men, but out of the numberless methods invented, are only puzzled which to choose … If indeed, any new and salutary mode of preserving life were discovered, such a discovery would not awaken the jealousy, nor become, in any degree, such a stimulus to the inventive faculties of other nations as the art of destruction, and the progress of such discoveries has always been slow and their salutary consequences remote and precarious. Inoculation was practiced in Turkey, long before it was known in Europe; and vaccination has, at this moment, many prejudices to contend with….

Atheism; the apostles of
The three great apostles of practical atheism, that make converts without persecuting, and retain them without preaching are Wealth, Health and Power.

Attacks; when to forgive
We most readily forgive that attack which affords us an opportunity of reaping a splendid triumph. A wise man will not sally forth from his doors to cudgel a fool, who is in the act of breaking his windows, by pelting them with guineas.

Authors; beware of egotism
The awkwardness and embarrassment which all feel on beginning to write, when they *themselves* are the theme, ought to serve as a hint to authors, that self is a subject they ought very rarely to descant upon. It is extremely easy to be as egotistical as Montigny, and as conceited as Rosseau; but it is extremely difficult to be as entertaining as the one, or as eloquent as the other.

Authors; posthumous evaluation
If an author writes better than his contemporaries, they will term him a plagiarist; if as well, a pretender; but if worse, he may stand some chance of commendation, a genius of some promise, from whom much may be expected, by a due attention to their good council and advice. When a dull author has arrived at this point, the best thing he can do for his fame, is to die before he can follow it. His brother dullards will in this case club their efforts to confer upon him one year of *immortality* a boon which few of them could realize for themselves; and this year of fame may be even extended to two, provided the candidate can be proved to have died on classic ground, and to have been buried within the verge of the meanderings of the Tiber, or the murmuring of the Melissus.

Authors (dead); enjoy advantages
The society of dead authors has this advantage over that of the living, they never flatter us to our faces, nor slander us behind our backs, nor intrude upon our privacy, nor quit their shelves until we take them down. Besides, it is always easy to shut a book, but not quite so easy to get rid of a lettered coxcomb. Living authors, therefore are usually bad companions; if they have not gained a character, they seek to do so by methods often ridiculous, always disgusting; and if they have established a character, they are silent for fear of losing by their tongue what they have acquired by their pen; for many authors converse much more foolishly than Goldsmith, who have never written half so well.

Authors (dull); our judgment, their conceit
Dull authors will measure our judgment not by our abilities, but by their own conceit. To admire their vapidity is to have superior taste; to despise it is to have none.

Avarice; dangers from
Avarice has ruined more men than prodigality, and the blindest thoughtlessness of expenditure has not destroyed so many fortunes, as the calculating but insatiable lust of accumulation.

Beauty; when perfect

That is not the most perfect beauty, which, in public, would attract the greatest observation; not even that which the statuary would admit to be a faultless piece of clay, kneaded up with blood. But that is true beauty, which has not only a substance, but a spirit — a beauty that we must intimately know, justly to appreciate — a beauty lighted up in conversation, where the mind shines as it were through its casket, where; in the language of the poet, *"the eloquent blood spoke in her cheeks, and so distinctly wrought that we might almost say her body thought."* An order and a mode of beauty which, the more we know, the more we accuse ourselves for not having before discovered those thousand graces which bespeak that their owner has a soul. This is that beauty which never cloys, possessing charms as resistless as those of the fascinating Egyptian for which Anthony wisely paid the bauble of a world, — a beauty like the rising of his own Italian suns, always enchanting never the same.

Beds; a paradox

Bed is a bundle of paradoxes; we go to it with reluctance, yet we quit it with regret; and we make up our minds every night to leave it early, but we make up our bodies every morning to keep it late.

Benevolence dictates, prudence confirms

As there is none so weak, that we venture to injure them with impunity, so there are none so *low* that they might at some time be able to repay an obligation. Therefore what benevolence would dictate, prudence would confirm. For he that is cautious of insulting the weakest, and not above obliging the lowest, will have attained such habits of forbearance and of complacency, as will secure him the good-will of all who are beneath him, and teach him how to avoid the enmity of all of those who are above him. For he that would not bruise even a worm, will be still more cautious how he treads upon a serpent.

Benevolence; requires economy

There is nothing that requires so strict an economy as our benevolence. We should husband our means as the agriculturist his manure, which if spread over too large a superficies produces no crop, if over too small a surface, exuberates in rankness and in weeds.

Bible vs. Sword; arguments

We should ridicule a general, who, just before an action, disarms his men, and putting into the hands of all of them, a bible, should order them, thus equipped, to march against the enemy. Here we plainly see the folly of calling in the bible to support the sword, but is it not as great a folly to call in the sword to support the bible?

Blackguards; do not argue with them

If you cannot avoid a quarrel with a blackguard, let your lawyer manage it, rather than yourself. No man sweeps his own chimney, but employs a chimney sweeper, who has no objection to dirty work, because it is his trade.

Books; danger in reading only scarce ones
He that will have no books but those that are scarce, evinces about as correct a taste in literature, as he would do in friendship, who would have no friends but those whom all of the rest of the world has sent to Coventry.

Charities: posthumous
Posthumous charities are the very essence of selfishness when bequeathed by those who, when alive, would part with nothing. In Catholic countries there is no mortmain act, and those, who, when dying, impoverish their relations, by leaving their fortunes to be expended in masses for themselves, have been shrewdly said so leave their own souls to their heirs.

Christian Fortitude and God's pleasure
Murmur at nothing; if our ills are reparable, it is ungrateful; if remediless, it is vain. But a Christian builds his fortitude on a better foundation than Stoicism; he is pleased with every thing that happens, because he knows it could not happen, unless it had first pleased God, and that which pleases him must be best. He is assured that no new thing can befall him and that he is in the hands of a Father who will prove him with no affliction that resignation cannot conquer or death cannot cure.

City Men; callous to others
In great cities men are more callous both to the happiness and misery of others, than in the country; for they are constantly in the habit of seeing both extremes.

Civil Law; its shortcomings
The great remora to any improvement in our civil code is the reduction that such reform must produce in the revenue. The laws' delays, bills of revival, rejoinder, and renewal empty the Stamp Office of stamps, and the pockets of the plaintiff and defendant of their money, but unfortunately they fill the Exchequer. Some one has said, that injustice, if it be speedy, would, in certain cases, be more desirable, than justice, if it be slow; and although we hear much of the glorious uncertainty of the law, yet all who have tried it will find, to their cost, that it can boast of two certainties, expense and delay....

Concessions; in matters of government
In great matters of public moment, where both parties are at a stand, and both are punctilious, slight condescensions cost little, but are worth much. He that yields them is wise in as much as he purchases guineas with farthings. A few drops of oil will set the political machine at work, when a ton of vinegar would only corrode the wheels and canker the movements.

Conduct of Corporate Bodies
The conduct of corporate bodies sometimes would incline one to suspect that criminality is, with them a matter of calculation, rather than of conscience, since the individuals that compose these bodies, provided they can only *divide* the weight of the odium attached to an obnoxious measure, have no objection to the *full* weight of the profit and the *whole* weight of the guilt....

Conquerors; the risks they run
Louis the Fourteenth, having become a king by the death of his minister, Mazarin, set up the trade of a conqueror, on his own account. The devil treated him as he does young gamesters, and bid very high for him; at first, by granting him unexampled success; he finished by punishing him with reverses equally unexampled. Thus, that sun which he had taken for his device, although it rose in cloudless majesty, was doomed to set in obscurity, tarnished by the smoke of his defeats, and tinged with the blood of his subjects.

Conversation with Sensible Men; warning
When we are in the company of sensible men we ought to be doubly cautious of talking too much, lest we lose two good things, their good opinion and our own improvement, and disclose one thing which had better been concealed, our self-sufficiency; for what we have to say we know, but what they have to say we know not.

Corruption; like a ball of snow
Corruption is like a ball of snow, when once set a rolling it must increase. It gives momentum to the activity of the knave, but it chills the honest man, and makes him almost weary of his calling; and all that corruption attracts, it also retains, for it is easier not to fall, than only to fall once, and not to yield a single inch than having yielded to regain it.

Courage; defined
Courage is generosity of the highest order, for the brave are prodigal of the most precious things. Our blood is nearer and dearer to us than our money; and our life than our estate.... In fact, true courage, well directed, can neither be over paid nor over praised. A hero is not composed of common materials; his expense is hazard, his coin is blood, and out of the very impossibilities of the coward, he cuts a perilous harvest, with his sword. We cannot aspire to so high a character, on cheaper terms, otherwise Falstaff's soldiers might be allowed their claim, since they were afraid of nothing but danger. It is unfortunate, however, that presence of mind is always most necessary, when absence of body would be most desirable; and there is this paradox in fear, he is most likely to inspire it in others, *who have none themselves.*

Courage; and the Fear of Death
Courage is incompatible with the fear of death; but every villain fears death; therefore no villain can be brave. He may, indeed, possess the courage of a rat, and fight with desperation, when driven into a corner.... Yet the glare of a courage thus elicited by danger, where fear conquers fear, is not to be compared to that calm sunshine which constantly cheers and illuminates the breast of him who builds his confidence on virtuous principle....

Cowardice: and the Love of Power
That cowardice is incorrigible which the love of power cannot overcome. In the heat and frenzy of the French revolution, the contentions for place and power, never sustained the smallest diminution; appointments and offices were never pursued with more eagerness and intrigue, than when the heads of those who gained them, had they been held on merely by pieces of *sticking plaster,* could not have sat more *loosely* on their shoulders. Demagogues sprung up like *mushrooms,* and it repeatedly happened that the guillotine had finished the favourite, before the plasterer had finished the model, and that the original was *dead* before the bust was *dry.*

Cuckoldom and Fame
What Fontenelle said of cuckoldom, might *more* truly be said of fame; it is nothing if you do not know it and very little if you do. Nor does the similarity end here; for in both cases, the principals, though first concerned, are usually the very parties that are last informed.

Death; as a liberator*
Death is the liberator of him whom freedom cannot release, the physician of him whom medicine cannot cure, and the comforter of him whom time cannot console.

Death; fear of*
Death is like thunder in two particulars; we are alarmed at the sound of it, and it is formidable only from that which preceded it. The rich man, gasping for breath, and reduced to be a mendicant even of the common air, tantalized with luxuries that must no more be tasted, and means that must no longer be enjoyed, feels at last the impotence of gold; and that death which he dreaded at a distance as an enemy, he now hails when he is near, as a friend; a friend that alone can bring the peace his treasures cannot purchase, and remove the pain his physicians cannot cure.

Death; many roads to*
In death itself there can be nothing terrible, for the act of death annihilates sensation; but there are many roads to death, and some of them justly formidable, even to the bravest, but so various are the modes of going out of the world, that to be born may have been more painful than to die, and to live may prove a more troublesome thing than either.
* See "Death, so misrepresented and abused." In Recycle Bin.

Debate; the art of
In answering an opponent, arrange your ideas, but not your words; consider in what points thing that resemble differ, and in what those things that differ, resemble; reply to wit with gravity and to gravity with wit; make a full concession to your adversary, and give him every credit for those arguments you know you can answer, and slur over all those which you feel you cannot; but above all, if he has the privilege of making his reply, take especial care that the strongest thing you have to urge is the last. He must immediately get up and say something and, if he be not previously prepared with an answer to your last argument, he will infallibly be boggled, for very few possess that remarkable talent of Charles Fox, who could talk on one thing, and at the same time think of another.

Defeat; when to accept
To excel others is a proof of talent; but to *know when* to conceal that superiority is a greater proof of prudence. The celebrated orator Domitius Afer, when attacked in a set speech by Caligula, made no reply, affecting to be entirely overcome by the resistless eloquence of the tyrant. Had he replied, he would certainly have conquered, and as certainly would have died; but he wisely preferred a defeat that *saved* his life to a *victory* that would cost it.

Deliberate with Caution
Deliberate with caution, but act with decision; and yield with graciousness, or oppose with firmness.

Depravity and the priests
The depravity of human nature is a favourite topic with the priests, but they will not brook that the laity should descant upon it; in this respect they may be compared to those husbands who freely abuse their own wives, but are ready to cut the throat of any other man who does so.

Designing Men and small favours
Many designing men, by asking small favours, and evincing great gratitude, have eventually obtained the most important ones. There is something in the human mind (perhaps the force of habit) which strongly inclines us to continue to oblige those whom we have begun to oblige and to injure those whom we have begun to injure.

Despotism; freedom of the press
Despotism can no more exist in a nation, until the liberty of the press be destroyed, then the night can happen before the sun is set.

Dining with the Great
He that likes a hot dinner, a warm welcome, *new* ideas, and *old* wine, will not often dine with the great.

Diogenes; his search for an honest man
If Diogenes used a lantern in broad daylight solely and simply for the purpose of discovering an honest man, this proceeding was not consistent with usual sagacity. A lantern would have been a more appropriate appendage, if he had been in search of a *rogue,* for such characters skulk about in holes and corners, and hate the light, because their deeds are evil. But I suspect this philosopher's real motive for using a lantern in mid-day, was to provoke inquiry, that he might have the cynical satisfaction of telling all that asked him what he was searching for, that none of them were the men to his mind, and that his search had hitherto been fruitless. It is with honesty in one particular, as with wealth, those that have the thing, care less about the credit of it, than those who have it not. No poor man can well afford to be thought so, and the less of honesty a finished ro possesses, the less he can afford to be supposed to want it....

Disputes and Personalities
Some have wondered that disputes about opinions should so often end in personalities but the fact is, that such disputes begin with personalities, for our opinions are a part of our selves.

Dogmatism; and its reverse
If it be true, that men of strong imaginations are usually dogmatists, and I am inclined to think it is so, it ought to follow that men of weak imagination are the reverse; in which case, we should have some compensations for stupidity. But it unfortunately happens that no dogmatist is more obstinate, or less open to conviction than a fool. And the only difference between the two would seem to be this, the former is

determined to force his knowledge upon others; the latter is equally determined that others shall not force their knowledge upon him.

Doubt; a vestibule to wisdom
Doubt is the vestibule which *all* must pass, before they can enter into the temple of wisdom; therefore, when we are in doubt, and puzzle out the truth by our own exertions, we have gained something that will stay by us and will serve us again. But, if to avoid the trouble of the search, we avail ourselves of the superior information of a friend, such knowledge will not remain with us; we have not *bought* but *borrowed* it.

Dressing beyond Their Means
It is not every man that can *afford* to wear a shabby coat; and *worldly* wisdom dictates to *her* disciples, the propriety of dressing somewhat beyond their means, but of living somewhat within them; for every one sees how we dress, but none sees how we live, except we choose to let them. But the truly great are, by universal suffrage, exempted from these trammels, and may live or dress, as they please.

Drinking and Gaming; public policy
The policy of drawing public revenue from the private vices of drinking, and of gaming, is as purblind as it is pernicious; for temperate men drink the most, because they drink the longest. And the gamester contributes much less to the revenue than the industrious because he is much sooner ruined. When Mandeville maintained that private vices were public benefits, he did not calculate the widely destructive influence of bad example. To affirm that a vicious man is only his *own* enemy, is about as wise as to affirm that a virtuous man is only his *own friend.*

Drunkenness; a vice of a good constitution
Drunkenness is the vice of a good constitution or a bad memory; of a constitution so treacherously good that it never bends until it breaks; or of a memory that recollects the pleasures of getting drunk, but forgets the pains of getting sober.

Duelling; revenge or fear?
No duels are palatable to both parties, except those that are engaged in from motives of revenge. Such duels are rare in modern times, for law has been found as efficacious for this purpose, as lead, though not so expeditious, and the lingering tortures inflicted by parchment, as terrible as the more summary decisions of the pistol. In all affairs of honour, excepting those where the sole motive is revenge, it is curious that fear is the main ingredient. From fear we accept a challenge, and from fear we refuse it. From the false fear of opinion we enter the lists, or we decline to do so, from the real fear of danger, or the moral fear of guilt. Dueling is an evil that will be extremely difficult to eradicate, because it would require a society composed of such materials as are not to be found without admixture, a society where all who are not Christians, must at least be gentlemen, or, if neither — then philosophers.

Duels; seconds vs. principals

If all seconds were as adverse to duels as their principals, very little blood would be shed in that way.

Dunces (learned)

It is curious that some learned dunces, because they can write nonsense in languages that are dead, should despise those that can talk sense in languages that are living. To acquire a few tongues, is the task of a few years, but to be eloquent in one, is the labour of a life.

Duties; delegation of

They that are in power should be extremely cautious to commit the execution of their plans, not only to those who are *able*, but to those who are *willing*; as servants and instruments it is their duty to do their best, but their employers are never as sure of them as when their duty is also their *pleasure*. To commit the execution of a purpose, to one who disapproves of the plan of it, is to employ but *one third* of the man; his heart and his head are against you, you have commanded only his hands.

Effrontery; as a substitute for courage
There is hardihood of effrontery, which will, under many circumstances, supply the place of courage, as impudence has sometimes passed current for wit. Wilkes had much of the first, and Mirabeau of the second. He received challenge after challenge, but unlike Wilkes, he accepted none of them, and contented himself merely writing down the names of the parties in his pocket book. It is not fair, he would say, that a man of talent like myself should be exposed to blockheads like these. It would seem that he had argued himself into the same kind of self importance with Rosseau, who came to this very disinterested conclusion, that it was incumbent upon him to take the most possible care of Jean Jacques (Rosseau) for the good of society.

Eloquence; the art of
In addressing the multitude, we must remember to follow the advice that Cromwell gave his soldiers, *"fire low"* This is the great art of the Methodists, *"fas est et ab hoste doceri"** If our eloquence be directed above the heads of our hearers, we shall do no execution. By pointing our arguments *low*, we stand a chance of hitting their *hearts*, as well as their *heads*. In addressing angels we could hardly raise our eloquence too high; but we must remember that men are not angels. Would we warm *them* by our eloquence, *unlike* Mahomet's mountain, it must come down to them, since they cannot raise themselves to it. It must come home to their wants and their wishes, to their hopes and their fears, to their families and their firesides. The moon gives a far greater light than *all* the fixed stars put together, although she is much smaller than any of them; the reason is that the stars are superior and remote; but the moon is *inferior* and *contiguous*.
* "It is wise to learn from our enemies".

Emulation vs. Envy
Emulation looks out for merits that she may exalt herself by a victory. Envy spies out blemishes, that she may lower another by a defeat.

Enemies; how to get them
If you want enemies, excel others; if you want friends, let others excel you. There is a diabolical trio existing in the *natural* man, implacable, inextinguishable, co-operative and consentaneous: Pride; Envy and Hate; Pride, that makes us fancy we deserve all the goods that others possess; Envy, that some should be admired, while we are overlooked; and Hate, because all that is stowed on others, diminishes the sum that we think due to ourselves.

Enemies; who are to be pitied
There are some men whose enemies are to be pitied much and their *friends* more.

England; predictions of her downfall
England can bear more mismanagement, luxury, and corruption, than any other nation under heaven; and those who have built their predictions of her downfall from analogies taken from other nations, have all fortunately failed, because England has

four points of strength and reviviscence, not common to those examples from which these analogies have been drawn. Two of these sources of strength are *physical*, her coal and her iron; and two of them are *moral;* the freedom of the press, and the trial by jury; and they are mutually conservative of each other, for should any attempt be made to destroy the two last, the two first are admirably adapted to defend them.

Envious; their censure
The praise of the *envious* is far less creditable than their *censure*; they praise only that which they can surpass; that surpasses them — they censure.

Envy; like a scorpion
Envy, if surrounded on all sides by the brightness of another's prosperity, like the scorpion, confined within a circle of fire will sting *itself* to death.

Error; one that all commit
To judge by the event, is an error all abuse, and all commit; for, in every instance, courage, if crowned with success, is heroism; if clouded by defeat, temerity. When Nelson fought his battle in the Sound, it was the result *alone* that decided whether he was to kiss a *hand* at a court, or a *rod* at a court-martial.

Evil; how it increases and multiplies
It is astonishing how parturescent is evil, and with what incestuous fertility the whole family of vice increase and multiply, by cohabiting amongst themselves. Thus, if kings are tyrannical and oppressive, it is too often because subjects are servile and corrupt. In proportion to the cowardice of the ruled, is the cruelty of the ruler, and if he governs by threats and by bribes, rather than by justice and by mercy, it is because fear has a stronger influence over the base than love and gain more weight with the mercenary, than gratitude. Thus the gladiatorial shows of ancient Rome, brought upon the institutors of them, their own punishment; for cruelty begat cruelty. The tyrant exercised those barbarities on the people, which the people exercised upon the prisoner and the slave; the physical value of man fell with his morals, and a contempt for the lives of others, was bred in all, by a familiarity with blood.

Evils; when most dreaded
Evils are more to be dreaded from the suddenness of their attack, than from their magnitude, or their duration. In the storms of life, those that are foreseen are half overcome, but the typhoon is a just cause of alarm to the helmsman, pouncing on a vessel, as an eagle on the prey.

Examinations
Examinations are formidable, even to the best prepared, for the greatest fool may ask more than the wisest man can answer.

Experience; better to borrow than to buy

"*Felix quem faciunt aliena pericula cautum*"* this is well translated by some one who observes that it is far better to *borrow* experience than to *buy* it. He that sympathizes in all the happiness of others, perhaps himself enjoys the safest happiness, and he that is warned by all the folly of others has perhaps attained the soundest wisdom. But such is the purblind egotism and the suicidal selfishness of mankind, that things so desirable are seldom pursued, things so accessible, seldom attained. That is indeed a *twofold* knowledge which profits alike, by the folly of the foolish, and the wisdom of the wise; it is both a shield and a sword; it borrows its security from the darkness, and its confidence from the light.

* Happy whom other's dangers make prudent.

Failings in Others, Not in Ourselves
What we conceive to be failings in others, are not infrequently owing to some deficiencies in ourselves; thus, plain men think handsome women want passion, and plain women think young men want politeness; dull writers think all readers devoid of taste, and dull readers think witty writers devoid of brilliance; old men can see nothing to admire in the present days; and yet former days were not better, but it is they themselves that have become worse.

Fame; an undertaker
Fame is an undertaker that pays but little attention to the living, but bedizens the dead, furnishes out their funerals, and follows them to the grave.

Fashion; the queen of fools*
The minor miseries super induced by Fashion, that queen of fools, can hardly be conceived by those who live in the present day, when common sense is invalidating every hour the authority of this silly despot, and confirming the rational dictates of comfort. The quantum of uneasiness forced upon us by these absurdities, was no small drawback from the subtotal of that happiness allotted to the little life of man; for small miseries, like small debts, hit us in so many places, and meet us at so many turns and corners, that what they want in weight, they make up in number and render it less hazardous to stand the fire of one cannon ball, than a volley composed of such a shower of bullets.
* See "Fashion, dictates of" in the Recycle Bin

Fate of the Fallen Woman
Women do not transgress the bounds of decorum as often as men; but when they do, they go to greater lengths. For with reason somewhat weaker, they have to contend with passions somewhat stronger; besides, a female by *one* transgression, forfeits her place in society forever; if once she falls, it is the fall of Lucifer. It is hard, indeed, that the law of opinion should be most severe on that sex which is least able to bear it, but so it is, and if the sentence be harsh, the sufferer should be reminded that it was passed by her *peers*. Therefore, if once a woman breaks through the barriers of decency, her case is desperate, and if she goes greater lengths than the man, and leaves the pale of propriety *farther behind her* it is because she is aware that all return is prohibited, and by none so strongly as by her own sex. We may also add that as modesty is the richest ornament of a woman, the want of it is her greatest deformity, for the better the thing, the worse will ever be its perversion; and if an *angel* falls the *transition* must be to a daemon.

Faults; two kinds, right and safe
As there are some faults that have been termed faults on the right side; so there are some errors that might be denominated errors on the *safe* side. Thus, we seldom regret having been too mild, too cautious, or too humble, but we often repent having been too violent, precipitate or too proud.

Favouritism; can cause injury
We may concede any man a right, without doing any man a wrong, but we can favour no one, without injuring some one. Where there are many claimants and we select one for his superior merits, this is a preference, and to this preference he has a right; but if we make our election from any other motive, this is a partiality, and this partiality although it may be a benefit to him, is a wrong to another. We may be very active, and very busy, but if strict justice be not the rudder of all our other virtues, the faster we sail, the farther we shall find ourselves from *"that haven where we would be"*.

Fear; debilitates, hope animates
Fear debilitates and lowers, but hope animates and revives; therefore rulers and magistrates should attempt to operate on the minds of their respective subjects, if possible, by reward, rather than punishment. And this principle will be strengthened by another consideration; he that is punished or rewarded, while he falls or rises in the estimation of others, cannot fail to do so likewise in his own.

Flattery; a traffic of mutual meanness
Flattery is often a traffic of mutual meanness, where, although both parties intend deception, neither is deceived; since words that cost little, are exchanged for hopes that cost less. But we must be careful how we flatter fools too little, or wise men too much, for the flatterer must act the very reverse of the physician, and administer the strongest dose, only to the *weakest* patient. The truly great will bear even reproof, if truth supports it, more patiently than flattery accompanied with falsehood; for by venturing on the first, we pay a compliment to their heart, but by venturing on the second, we inflict an insult on their head.

Flattery; by use of abuse
Adroit observers will find that some who affect to dislike flattery, may yet be flattered indirectly, by a well seasoned abuse and ridicule of their rivals. Diogenes professed to be no flatterer; but his cynic raillery was, in other words, flattery; it fed the ruling passion of the Athenian mob, who was more pleased to hear their superiors abused, than themselves commended.

Flattery of the Great; stale and a glut
There is a very cunning flattery, which great minds some times pay them, by condescending to admire efforts corresponding with, but vastly inferior to their own. This will help lose observers to account for a vast deal of otherwise unaccountable flummery that is hawked about in the market of fame, but very cheap like all other articles, that are so doubly unfortunate as to be not only stale, but a glut.

Fools; memory and resentment
Strong and sharp as our wit may be, it is not so strong as the memory of fools, nor so keen as their resentment; he that has not strength of mind to forgive, is by no means so weak as to forget; and it is more easy to do a cruel thing, than to say a severe one.

Fools and Rogues; what they know
Every fool knows how often he has been a rogue, but every rogue does not know how often he has been a fool.

Fortune; guardian of fools
Fortune has been considered the guardian divinity of fools; and, on this score, she has been accused of blindness; but it should be adduced as a proof of her sagacity, when she helps those who certainly cannot help themselves.

Fortunes; how to spend
If some persons were to bestow the one half of their fortune in learning how to spend the other half, it would be money extremely well laid out. He that spends two fortunes and permitting himself to be twice ruined, and dies at last a beggar, deserves no commiseration. He has gained neither experience from trial, nor repentance from reprieve. He has been all his life abusing fortune, without enjoying her, and purchasing wisdom, without possessing her.

Fraud and Stupidity
There are some frauds so well conducted, that it would be stupidity *not* to be deceived by them. A wise man, therefore, may be duped as well as a fool; but the fool publishes the triumph of his deceiver; and the wise man is silent, and denies that triumph to an enemy which he would hardly concede to a friend; a triumph that proclaims his own defeat.

Frauds; can succeed with candour
Some frauds succeed from the apparent candour, the open confidences, and the full blaze of ingenuousness that is thrown around them. The slightest mystery would excite suspicion, and ruin all. Such stratagems may be compared to the stars, they are discoverable by *darkness*, and hidden only by *light*.

Freedom of the press: useful to ruler
A king of England has an interest in preserving the freedom of the press, because it is to his interest to know the true state of the nation, which the courtiers would fain conceal, but of which a free press alone can inform him.

Friends and Jealousy
Our very best friends have a tincture of jealousy even in their friendship; and when they hear us praised by others, will ascribe it to sinister and interested motives if they can.

Friendships; formed by adversity
The finest friendships have been formed in mutual adversity, as iron is most strongly united by the fiercest flame.

Friendship vs. Love
Friendship often ends in love; but love, in friendship — never.

Friends vs. Enemies
An act, by which we make one friend, and one enemy, is a losing game; because revenge is a much stronger principle than gratitude.

Friends Who Abuse Their Wives or Their Horses
Never join with your friend when he abuses his horse or his wife, unless the one is about to be *sold* and the other to be *buried.*

French; their hate for other nations
The French nation despises all other nations, except the English; we have the honour of her hate, only because she cannot despise us.

French Revolution; description of
The French Revolution was a machine invented and constructed for the purpose of manufacturing liberty; but it had neither lever-clogs, nor adjusting powers, and the consequences were that it worked so rapidly that it destroyed its own inventors, and set itself on fire.

Funerals; pomposity and vanity
Those who bequeath unto themselves a pompous funeral, are at just so much expense to inform the world of something that had much better have been concealed; namely, that their vanity has survived themselves.

Gamester; doubly ruined
The gamester, if he dies a martyr to his profession, is doubly ruined. He adds his soul to every other loss, and by the act of suicide, renounces the earth, to forfeit heaven.

Gaming; child of avarice
Gaming is the child of avarice, but the parent of prodigality.

Genius; and the law of parturition
With the offspring of genius, the law of parturition is reversed; the throes are in the conception, the pleasure in the birth.

Gifts; disinterested
The most *disinterested* of all gifts, are those which kings bestow on *undeserving* favourites; first, because they are purely at the expense of the donor's *character;* and secondly, because they are sure to be repaid with ingratitude....

Generals; how they act
It has been said, that the retreat shows the general, as the reply the orator; and it is partly true; although a general would rather build his fame on his advances; than on his retreats, and on what he has attained, rather than on what he has abandoned. Moreau, we know, was famous for his retreats, in so much that his companions in arms compared him to a *drum*, which nobody hears of, *except it be beaten.* But, it is nevertheless true, that the merits of a general are not to be appreciated by the battle alone, but by those dispositions that preceded it, and by those measures that followed it. Hannibal knew better how to conquer, than how to profit by the conquest; and Napoleon was more skilful in taking positions, than in maintaining them. As to reverses, no general can presume to say that he may not be defeated; but he can; and ought to say, that he will not be surprised. There are dispositions so skilful, that the battle may be considered won, even before it is fought, and the campaign to be decided, even before it is contested. There are generals who have accomplished more by the march, than by the musket and Europe saw, in the lines of Torres Vedras, a simple telescope; in the hands of a Wellington, become an instrument, more fatal and destructive, than all the cannon in the camp of his antagonist.

God; on the side of virtue
God is on the side of virtue; for whoever dreads punishment, suffers it; and whoever deserves it, dreads it.

God Will Excuse Our Prayers For Ourselves
God will excuse our prayers for ourselves, whenever we are prevented from them, by being occupied in such good works as to entitle us the prayers of others.

Gold; its power
Those who worship gold in a world as corrupt as this we live in, have at least one thing to plead in defence of their idolatry — the power of their idol. It is true, that

like other idols, it can neither move, nor see, nor hear, nor feel, nor understand; but, unlike other idols, it has often communicated all these powers to those who had them not, and annihilated them in those who had. This idol can boast of two peculiarities; it is worshipped in all climates, without a single temple, and by all classes, without a single hypocrite.

Good and Evil; choosing between

The clashing interests of society, and the double, yet equal and contrary demands arising out of them, where duty and justice are constantly opposed to gratitude and inclination, these things must make the profession of a statesman, an office neither easy nor enviable. It often happens that such men have only a choice of evils, and that in adopting either, the discontent will be certain, the benefit precarious. It is seldom that statesmen have the option of choosing between a good and an evil; and still more seldom that they can boast of that fortunate situation, where, like the great Duke of Marlborough, they are permitted to choose between *two* things that are good. His Grace was hesitating whether he should take a prescription recommended by the duchess; "I will be hanged," said she, "If it does not cure you." Dr. Garth, who was present, instantly exclaimed. "Take it, then, Your Grace, by all manner of means; *it is sure to do good, one way or the other.*"

Good Deeds; the concealment of

If you have performed an act of great and disinterested virtue, conceal it, if you publish it, you will neither be believed *here,* nor rewarded *hereafter.*

Good Natured Humans; their fate

There are a vast number of easy, pliable, good-natured human expletives* in the world, who are just what the world chooses to make them; they glitter without pride, and are affable without humility; they sin without enjoyment, and pray without devotion; they are charitable, not to benefit the poor, but to court the rich; profligate without passion, they are debauchees to please others, and to punish themselves. Thus, a youth without fire, is followed by an old age without experience, and they continue to float down the tide of time, as circumstances or chance may dictate, divided between God and the world, and serving both, but rewarded by neither.
* Expletive "a person or thing that merely serves to take up space" Shorter Oxford English Dictionary Vol. I, p 706.

Goods of the World and Philosophers

With respect to goods of the world it might be said, that parsons are preaching for them — that lawyers are pleading for them — that physicians are prescribing for them — that authors are writing for them — that soldiers are fighting for them — but, that true philosophers alone are enjoying them.

Governments; kinds of

Of governments, that of the mob is the most sanguinary, that of soldiers the most expensive, and that of civilians the most vexatious.

Grant Graciously or Conciliate
Grant graciously what you cannot refuse safely, and conciliate those you cannot conquer.

Great Men; dark alleys of the heart
Great men, like great cities, have many crooked arts, and dark alleys in their hearts, whereby who knows them, may save him much time and trouble.

Great Men; why they receive so little pity
The reason why great men meet with so little pity or attachment in adversity would seem to be this. The friends of a great man were made by his fortunes, his enemies by himself, and revenge is a much more punctual paymaster than gratitude. Those whom a great man has marred, rejoice at his ruin. And those, whom he has made, look on with indifference; because, with common minds, the destruction of the creditor is considered as equivalent to the payment of the debt.

Great Possessions and Great Debt
There are two things that bestow consequences; great possessions or great debts.* Julius Caesar consented to be millions of sesterces worse than nothing. In order to be every thing; he borrowed large sums of his officers, to quell seditions in his troops, who had mutinied for want of pay, and thus forced his partisans to anticipate their own success only through that of their commander.
*The above remark is applicable to states, no less than to individuals. A public debt is a kind of an anchor in the storm, but if the anchor be too heavy for the vessel, she will be sunk by that very weight which was intended for her preservation.

Habit; will reconcile us, even to change
Habit will reconcile us to everything but change, and even to change, if it recur not too quickly. Milton, therefore, makes his hell an ice-house, as well as an oven, and freezes his devils, at one period, but bakes them at another. The late Sir George Staunton informed me that he had visited a man in India, who had committed a murder, and, in order not only to save his life, but what was of much more consequence, his *caste,* he submitted to the penalty imposed; this was, that he should sleep for seven years on a bedstead, without any mattress the whole surface of which was studded with points of iron resembling nails, but not so sharp as to penetrate the flesh. Sir George saw him in the fifth year of his probation, and his skin was then like the hide of a rhinoceros, but more callous; at that time, however, he could sleep comfortably on his "*bed of thorns*" and remarked, that at the expiration of the term of his sentence, he should most probably continue that system from choice, which he had been obliged to adopt from necessity.

Happiness; anticipation of*
Men spend their lives in anticipations, in determining to be vastly happy at some period or other, *when they have time.* But the present time has one advantage over every other — it is our own. Past opportunities are gone, future are not come. We may lay in a stock of pleasures, as we would lay in a stock of wine; but if we defer the tasting of them too long, we shall find that both are soured by age....
* See "Happiness and Growing Old" in the Recycle Bin.

Happiness and Misery*
In the constitution both of our mind and of our body, everything must go on right, and harmonize well together to make us happy, but should *one* thing go wrong, that is quite enough to make us miserable; and, although the joys of this world are vain and short, yet its sorrows are real and lasting, for I will show you a ton of perfect pain, with greater ease than one ounce of perfect pleasure; and he knows little of himself or of the world, who does not think it sufficient happiness to be free from sorrow; therefore, give a *wise* man health, and he will give himself every other thing. I say, give him health, for it often happens that the most ignorant empiric can do us the greatest harm, although the most skillful physician knows not how to do us the slightest good.
* See "Happiness and Growing Old" in the Recycle Bin

Happiness and Wisdom; the difference
There is this difference between happiness and wisdom; he that thinks himself the happiest man; really is so; but he who thinks himself the wisest, is generally the greatest fool.

Hate; the kind we all can bear
The hate which we all bear with the most Christian patience is the hate of those who envy us.

Hatred: differs from Pity
There is this difference between hatred and pity; pity is a thing often avowed, seldom felt; hatred is a thing often felt, seldom avowed.

Head of Party; requirements
He that aspires to be the head of a party will find it more difficult to please his friends than to perplex his foes. He must often act from false reasons which are weak, because he dares not avow the true reasons which are strong. It will be his lot to be forced on some occasions to give his consideration to the wealthy and the titled, although they may be in the *wrong,* and to withhold it from the energetic but necessitous, although they may be in the *right.* There are moments when he must appear to sympathize not only with the fears of the brave, but also with the follies of the wise. He must see some appearances that do not exist, and be blind to some that do. To be above others, he must condescend at times to be beneath himself, as the loftiest trees have the lowest roots. But without the keenest circumspection, his very *rise* will be his *ruin.* For a masked battery is more destructive than one that is visible, and he will have more to dread from the secret envy of his adherents, than the open hate of his adversaries. This envy will be ever near him, but he must not appear to suspect it; it will narrowly watch him, but he must not appear to perceive it; even when he is anticipating all its effect he must give no note of preparation, and in defending himself against it, must conceal both his sword and his shield. Let him pursue success as his truest friend, and apply to confidence as his ablest counsellor. Subtract from a great man all that he owes to opportunity, and all that he owes to chance, all that he has gained by the wisdom of his friends, and by the folly of his enemies and our Brobdignag will often become a Lilliputian.

Health vs. Money; difference
There is this difference between those two temporal blessings, health and money; money is the most envied, but the least enjoyed; health is the most enjoyed, but the least envied and this superiority of the latter is still more obvious, when we reflect that the poorest man would not part with health for money, but that the richest would gladly part with all their money for health.

Health vs. Wealth; the loss of either
How happens it that all men envy us our wealth, but that no man envies us our health. The reason perhaps is this; it is very seldom that we can lose our wealth, without some one being the better for it, by gaining that which we have lost; but no one is jealous of us, on account of our health, because if we were to lose that, this would be a loss that betters no one.

He Who Can Please Nobody
He that can please nobody is not so much to be pitied, as he that nobody can please.

History; the price we pay to know it
The more we know of History, the less shall we esteem the subjects of it, and to despise our species, is the price we must too often pay for our knowledge of it.

Honesty; the loss of
Some men commence life in a career of honesty, but meet with so many disappointments that they are obliged to disrobe themselves of their conscience, for fear it should grow as threadbare as their coat. *"Declinant cursus, aurumque volubile tollunt"** This is a degradation that will happen to most men, whose principles are rooted only on earth, unrefreshed by the dews of heaven. Such men begin well, but end ill; like a certain lawyer, who on being asked why he defended so many bad causes, replied that he did so, because he had lost so many good ones.
* "They that shun the race and snatch the slippery gold."

Horses, Dogs and Friends; the loss of
When we have lost a favourite horse or dog, we usually endeavour to console ourselves by the recollection of some bad qualities they happened to possess; and we are very apt to tranquillize our minds by similar reminiscences, on the deaths of those friends who have left us *nothing*.

Human minds; elasticity of
There is elasticity in the human mind, capable of bearing much, but which will not show itself, until a certain weight of affliction be put upon it; its powers may be compared to those vehicles whose springs are so contrived that they get on smoothly enough when loaded, but jolt confoundedly when they have *nothing to bear.*

Hurry Differs from Dispatch
No two things differ more than hurry and dispatch. Hurry is the mark of a weak mind, dispatch of a strong one. A weak man in office, like a squirrel in a cage, is labouring eternally, but to no purpose and in constant motion without getting on a jot; like a turnstile, he is in everybody's way, but stops nobody; he talks a great deal, but says very little, looks into every thing, but sees into nothing, and has a hundred irons in the fire, but very few of them are hot, and with those few that are, he only burns his fingers.

Husbands and Cuckoldom
Husbands cannot be *principals* in their own cuckoldom, but they are *parties* to it much more often than they themselves imagine.

Hypochondriacs; described
Those hypochondriacs, who, like Herodius, give up their whole time and thought to the care of their health, sacrifice unto life every noble purpose of living; striving to support a frail and feverish being here, they neglect a hereafter; they continue to patch up and repair their moldering tenement of clay, regardless of the immortal

tenant that must survive it; agitated by greater fears than the apostle, and supported by none of his hopes they "die daily".

Ignorance vs. Error
It is almost as difficult to make a man unlearn his *errors* as his knowledge. Mal-information is more hopeless than non-information; for error is always more busy than ignorance. Ignorance is a blank sheet on which we may write, but error is a scribbled one on which we must first erase. Ignorance is contented to *stand still* with her back to the truth; but error is more presumptuous, and *proceeds* in the *same* direction. Ignorance has no light, but error follows a false one. The consequence is, that error, when she retraces her footsteps, has farther to go, before she can arrive at the truth, than ignorance.

Imitation; the sincerest form of flattery
Imitation is the sincerest form of flattery.

Impotence of the Rich
It is only when the rich are sick, that they fully feel the impotence of wealth.

Injuries Accompanied by Insults; results
Injuries accompanied with insults are never forgiven; all men, on these occasions, are good haters, and lay out their revenge at compound interest. They never threaten until they can strike, and smile when they cannot. Caligula told Valerius *in public* what kind of a bed fellow his wife was; and when the Tribune Chereus, who had an effeminate voice, came to him for the watchword, would always give him Venus or Priapus. The first of these men was the principal instrument in the conspiracy against him, and the second cleft him down with his sword, to convince him of his manhood.

Injuries; by the weak and to the strong
It is easier to forgive the *weak*, who have injured *us,* than the *powerful* that *we* have injured. That conduct will be continued by our *fears*, which commenced in our resentment. He that has gone so far as to cut the claws of the lion will not feel himself quite secure, until he has also drawn his teeth. The greater the power of him that is injured, the more inexpiable must be the efforts of those, who have begun to injure him. Therefore a monarch, who submits to a single insult, is half dethroned. When the conspirators were deliberating on the murder of Paul Petrowitz, a voice was heard in the anti-chamber, saying, *"You have broken the egg; you had better make the omelet"*.

Injuring the Weak; results
As there are none so weak, that we may venture to injure them with impunity, so there are none so *low* that they may not at some time be able to repay an obligation. Therefore what benevolence would dictate, prudence would confirm. For he that is cautious of insulting the weakest, and not above obliging the lowest, will have attained such habits of forbearance and of complacency, as will secure him the good-will of all that are beneath him, and teach him how to avoid the enmity of all that are above him. For he that would not even bruise a worm, will be still more cautious how he treads upon a serpent.

Innovation; beware of

We ought not to be over anxious to encourage innovation, in cases of *doubtful* improvement, for an old system must ever have two advantages over a new one; it is established, and it is understood.

Integrity in Dealing; a warning

If you have cause to suspect the integrity of one with whom you *must* have dealings, take care to have no communication with him, if he has his friend, and you have not; you are playing a dangerous game, in which the odds are two to one against you.

Intimacy of the Great

He that can enjoy the intimacy of the great, and on no occasion disgust them by familiarity, or disgrace himself by servility, proves that he is as perfect a gentleman by nature, as his companions are by rank.

Invention of the Plough

It is not known where he that invented the plough was born, nor where he died; yet he has effected more for the happiness of the world, than the whole race of heroes and of conquerors, who have drenched it with tears, and manured it with blood, and whose birth, parentage, and education have been handed down to us with a precision precisely proportionate to the mischief they have done.

Jealousy; service and wages
Of all the passions, jealousy is that which exacts the hardest service, and pays the bitterest wages. Its service is — to watch the *success* of our enemy, — its wages —to be *sure* of it.

Jurisprudence vs. Justice
In civil jurisprudence it too often happens that there is so much law that there is no room for justice, and that the claimant expires of wrong, in the midst of right, as mariners die of thirst in the midst of water.

Kings; how they are treated by their people
The good people of England do all that in them lies to make their king a puppet; and then with their usual consistency, detest him if he is not what they would make him, and despise him if he is.

Kings and Happiness
If kings would only determine not to extend their dominions, until they had filled them with happiness, they would find the smallest territories too large, but the longest life too short for the full accomplishment of so grand and so noble an ambition.

Knaves; and those they cheat
A thoroughly paced knave will rarely quarrel with one whom he can cheat; his revenge is plunder; therefore he is usually the most forgiving of beings, upon the principle that if he comes to an open rupture, he must defend himself, and this does not suit a man whose vocation it is to keep his hands in the pockets of another.

Ladies; happiness and love
Ladies of Fashion starve their happiness to feed their vanity; and their love to feed their pride.

Laws and Arms
In all governments, there must of necessity be both the law and the sword; laws without arms would give us not liberty, but license; and arms without laws, would produce not subjection, but slavery. The law, therefore, should be unto the sword, what the handle is to the hatchet; it should direct the stroke, and temper the force.

Laws of England; criminal and civil are the best
England, with a criminal code the most bloody, and a civil code the most expensive in Europe, can, notwithstanding, boast of more happiness and freedom than any other country under Heaven. The reason is that despotism and all its minor ramifications of discretionary power, lodged in the hands of individuals, is utterly unknown.

Law and Equity
Law and equity are two things which God hath joined, but which man hath put asunder.

Laws that are too severe
Laws that are too severe, are temptations to plunder on the part of the criminal, and to perjury on the part of the prosecutor, since he would rather burden his conscience with a false oath; than with a true one, which would arm cruelty to kill, in the garb of justice. Such laws, therefore, reverse the natural order of things, transferring the indignation of public feeling which ought to follow the criminal, to the ferocity of that sentence by which he is to suffer, and taking from legislation its main support, the sympathy of public esteem and approbation; for the victim to too severe a law is considered as a martyr, rather than a criminal, and that which we pity, we cannot at the same time detest.

Learning vs. Instructing
It is always safe to learn, even from our enemies — seldom safe to venture to instruct, even our friends.

Liberties; taking them, with great men
It is dangerous to take liberties with great men, unless we know them thoroughly; the keeper will hardly put his head into the lion's mouth, upon a *short* acquaintance.

Life; enjoyment of
How small a portion of our life is that we really enjoy. In youth we are looking forward to things that are to come; in old age, we are looking backwards to things that are gone past; in things that are present, yet even that is too often absorbed in vague determinations to be vastly happy on some future day, when we have time.

Life; a theatre
In all societies it is advisable to associate if possible with the highest; not that the highest are always the best, but, because if disgusted there, we can always descend; — but if we begin with the lowest, to ascend is impossible. In the grand theatre of human life, a *box ticket* takes us through the house.

Life-taking: by the powerful and the weak
The worst thing that can be said of the powerful is; that they can take your life; but the same thing can be said of the most weak.

Literature: how we judge it
In literature our taste will be discovered by that which we give and our judgment by that which we withhold.

Literature; pioneers in dirt and rubbish
He that shortens the road to knowledge, lengthens life, and we are all of us more indebted than we believe we are to that class of writers whom Johnson termed the "pioneers of literature, doomed to clear away the dirt and the rubbish, for those heroes who press on to honour and to victory without deigning to bestow a single smile on the humble drudge that facilitates their progress".

Literature and Great Men
As in literature we shall find many things that are true, and some things that are new, but very few things that are both true and new, so also in life, we shall find many men that are great, and some men that are good, but very few men that are both great and good....

Little Men; described
The most disagreeable two-legged animal I know is a little great man, and the next, a little great man's factotum and friend.

Little Men and Mischief
To know exactly how much mischief may be ventured upon with impunity is knowledge sufficient for a *little* great man.

Living; city vs. village
If you would be known, and not know, *vegetate* in a village, if you would know, and not be known, *live* in a city.

Living alone; benefits of
Those who have resources within themselves, who can dare to live alone, want friends the least, but, at the same time, best know how to prize them the most. But no company is far preferable to bad, because we are more apt to catch the vices of others than their virtues, as disease is far more contagious than health.

Living alone; takes the rarest courage
Expense of thought is the rarest prodigality, and to dare to live alone the rarest courage; since there are many who had rather meet their bitterest enemy in the field, than their own hearts in their closet. He that has no resources of mind is more to be pitied than he who is in want of necessaries for the body, to be obliged to beg our daily happiness from others, bespeaks a more lamentable poverty than that of him who begs his daily bread.

Logic as an Instrument
Logic is a large drawer, containing some useful instruments, and many more that are superfluous. But a wise man will look into it for two purposes, to avail himself of those instruments that are really useful, and to admire the ingenuity with which those that are not so, are assorted and arranged.

London; he who tires of London, tires of life
Doctor Johnson was not far from the truth, when he observed, that he could sit in the smoky corner of Bolt Court, and draw a circle round himself, of one mile in diameter, that should comprise and embrace more energy, ability and intellect, than could be found in the whole island besides. The circumstance of talent of every kind being so accessible, in consequence of its being so contiguous, this it is that designates London as the real university of England. If we wish to collate *manuscripts*, we may repair to Oxford or to Cambridge, but we must come to London if we wish to collate *men*.

Long Life; its effect
Many who find the day too long, think life too short; but short as life is, some find it long enough to outlive their characters, their constitutions and their estates.

Long Life vs. Improved Life
It is astonishing how much more anxious people are to lengthen life than to improve it; and as misers often lose large sums of money in attempting to make more, so do hypochondriacs squander large sums of time in search of nostrums by which, they vainly hope they may get more time to squander. Thus the journals give us ten thousand recipes to live long, for one to live well, and hence the use of that present we now have, is thrown away in idle schemes of how we shall abuse that future we may not have. No man can promise himself even fifty years of life, but any man may, if he please, live the proportion of fifty years, in forty — let him rise early, that he may have the day before him, and let him make the most of the day, by determining to expend it on *two* sorts of acquaintances only, those from something may be got, and those from whom something may be learnt.

Long Marches and Tight Shoes
He that undertakes a long march should not have tight shoes, or he that undertakes great measures, tight manacles. In order to save all, it is sometimes necessary to risk all. To risk less would be to lose the whole, since half would be swallowed up by those who have deserted us, and the other half by those who have defeated us.

Love; gratitude as an ally to
It is a dangerous experiment to call in gratitude as an ally to love. Love is a debt, which inclination always pays, obligation never, and the moment it becomes lukewarm, and evanescent, reminiscences on the score of gratitude, serve only to smother the flame, by increasing the fuel.

Love; the power of
The power of love consists mainly in the privilege that Potentate possesses of coining, circulating, and making current those falsehoods between man and woman that would not pass for one moment, either between woman and woman, or man and man.

Love of Women
If you cannot inspire a woman with love of you, fill her above the brim with love of herself — all that runs over will be yours.

Love without Jealousy
Love may exist without jealousy, although this rare; but jealousy may exist without love, and this is common, for jealousy can feed on that, which is bitter, no less than on that which is sweet, and is sustained by pride, as often as by affection.

Mahomet; use of promises
None knew how to draw long bills on futurity that never will be honoured, better than prophet Mahomet. He possessed himself of a large stock of real and present pleasure and power here, by promising a visionary quantum of those good things to his followers hereafter; and, like the maker of an almanac made his fortune in this world, by telling absurd lies about another.

Marriage is a Feast
Marriage is a feast where the grace is sometimes better than *the dinner.*

Martyrs to Vice
The martyrs to vice far exceed the martyrs to virtue, both in endurance and in number. So blinded are we by our passions, that we suffer more to be damned than to be saved.

Martyrdom; proves what?
He that dies a martyr proves that he was not a knave, but by no means that he was not a fool; since the most absurd doctrines are not without such evidence as martyrdom can produce. A martyr, therefore, by the *mere* act of suffering, can prove nothing but his own faith. If, as was the case of the primitive Christian martyrs, it should clearly appear that the sufferer could not have been himself deceived, then, indeed, the evidence rises high, because the act of martyrdom absolves him from the charge of willfully deceiving others.

Memory is the Friend of Wit
Memory is the friend of wit, but the treacherous ally of invention; and there are many books that owe their success to two things, the good memory of those who write them, and the bad memory of those who read them.

Memory vs. Judgment
Why is it that we so constantly hear men complain of their memory, but none of their judgment; is it that they are less ashamed of a short memory because they have heard that this is a failing of great wits, or it because nothing is more common than a fool with a strong memory, or more rare, than a man of sense with a weak judgment.

Men; beware of those of even temper
Always suspect a man, who affects great softness of manner, an unruffled evenness of temper, and enunciation studied, slow and deliberate. These things are all unnatural, and bespeak a degree of mental discipline into which he that has no purposes of craft or design to answer, can not submit to drill himself. The most successful knaves are usually of this description, as smooth as razors dipped in oil, and as sharp. They affect the innocence of the dove, which they have not, in order to hide the cunning of the serpent, which they have.

Men; four classes

There are four classes of men in the world; first, those whom every one would wish to talk to, and whom every one does talk to; these are that small minority that constitutes the great. Secondly, those whom no one wishes to talk to, and whom no one does talk to; these are that vast majority that constitutes the little. The third class is made up of those whom everybody talks of, but nobody talks to; these constitute the knaves; and the fourth is composed of those everybody talks to, but whom nobody talks of; and these constitute the fools.

Men of True Greatness vs. the Mediocrist

I think it is Warburton who draws a very just distinction between a man of true greatness, and a mediocrist. "If", says he, "you want to recommend yourself to the former, take care that he quits your society with a good opinion of *you; if* your object is to please the latter, take care that he leaves you with a good opinion of himself."

Men vs. Women; improvement of one improves the other

No improvement that takes place in either of the sexes can possibly be confined to itself; each is a universal to each, and the respective refinement of the one, will always be in reciprocal proportion to the polish of the other.

Men vs. Women; the Dawn of Women's Lib

Lady Mary Wortley Montague observed, that in the whole course of her long and extensive travels, she had found but two sorts of people, *men and women*. This simple remark was founded on no small knowledge of human nature; but, we might add, that even this distinction, narrow as it is, is *now* gradually disappearing; for some of our beaus are imitating the women, in everything that is little and some of our women are imitating the men, in every thing that is great. Miss Edgeworth and Madame de Stael have proved there is no *sex in style* and Madame La Roche-Jacqueli and the Duchess d'Augouleme have proved there is also *no sex in courage.* Barbarous or refined, in rags or in ruffles, at St. Giles's or St. James's, covered in the skins of quadrupeds, or the costly entrails of an insect, *we are in essentials the same.* We pursue the same goods and fly the same evils; we loathe and love, and hope and fear, from causes that differ little in themselves, but only in their circumstances and modifications.

Men Who Are Fortune's Favourites

There are some men who are fortune's favourites, and who, like cats, light forever upon their legs. Wilkes was one of these didappers* whom, if you had stripped naked, and thrown over Westminster bridge, you might have met on the very next day, with a bag wig on his head, a sword by his side, a laced coat upon his back, and money in his pocket.

* "Applied ludicrously to a person" (1589), The Shorter Oxford English Dictionary, Vol. I.

Mental Diseases; defined
It is with diseases of the mind, as with those of the body, we are half dead, before we understand our disorder, and half cured when we do.

Mental Pleasures; defined
Mental pleasures never cloy; unlike those of the body, they are increased by repetition; approved of by reflection, and strengthened by enjoyment.

Methodists; their doctrines
When the Methodists first decide on the doctrine they approve; and then choose such pastors as they know before hand, will preach no other; they act as wisely as a patient, who should send for a physician; and then prescribe to him what medicines he ought to advise.

Middle Class; they have the finest feelings
It is in the middle classes of society that all the finest feelings, and the most amiable propensities of our nature, do principally flourish and abound. For the good opinion of our fellow men is the strongest, though, not the purest motive to virtue. The privations of poverty render us too cold and callous, and the privileges of property, too arrogant and consequential to feel, the first places us beneath the influence of opinion — the second, above it.

Mind; habituated to intrigue and mystery
There are minds so habituated to intrigue and mystery in themselves, and so prone to expect it from others, that they will never accept of a plain reason for a plain fact, if it be possible to devise causes for it that are obscure, farfetched, and usually *not worth the carriage*. Like the miser of Berkshire who would ruin a good horse, to escape a turnpike, so these gentlemen ride their highbred theories to death in order to come at truth, through bypaths, lanes and alleys; while she herself is jogging quietly along, upon the high and beaten road of common sense....

Ministers; upright and corrupt
An upright minister asks, *what* recommends a man; a corrupt minister asks *who?*

Misfortunes; our own, when supportable
Most of our misfortunes are more supportable than the comments of our friends upon them.

Misfortunes; pity from others
For one man who sincerely pities our misfortunes, there are a thousand who sincerely hate our successes.

Money; its power and its weaknesses
To cure us of our immoderate love of gain, we should seriously consider how many goods there are that money will not purchase, and these the best, and how many evils

there are that money will not remedy, and these the worst. An ancient philosopher of Athens, where the property of the wealthy was open to the confiscations of the informer, consoled himself for the loss of his fortune by the following reflection; I have lost my money, and with it my cares; for when I was rich I was afraid of every poor man, but now that I am poor, every rich man is afraid of me.

Morality; doubtful

In cases of doubtful morality, it is usual to say, is there any harm in doing this? This question may sometimes be answered by asking ourselves another; is there any harm in letting it alone?

Noble Income, Nobly Expended
A noble income, nobly expended, is no common sight; it is far more easy to acquire a fortune like a knave, than to expend it, like a gentleman. If we exhaust our income in schemes of ambition we shall purchase disappointment; if in law, vexation; if in luxury, disease. What we lend we shall most probably lose; what we spend rationally, we shall enjoy; what we distribute to the deserving, we shall both enjoy and *retain*.

Nobility of Birth; limits to accomplishment
Nobility of birth does not always ensure a corresponding nobility of mind; if it did it would always act as a stimulus to noble actions; but it sometimes acts as a clog, rather than a spur. For the favour and consideration of our fellow-men, is perhaps the strongest incentive to intellectual exertion; but rank and title, unfortunately for the possessors of them, ensure that favour and consideration, even without exertion, that others hardly can obtain, by means of it. Therefore men high in rank, are sometimes low in acquirement, not so much from want of ability, as from want of application; for it is the nature of man, not to expend labour on those things that he can have without it, nor to sink a well, if he happen to be born upon the banks of a river. But we might as well expect the elastic muscularity of a Gladiator, without training, as the vigorous intellect of a Newton, without toil.

Nostalgia; defined
The pining to revisit their native land, peculiar to the Swiss, is termed *Nostalgia*, a word that signifies a strong desire to return. They have been known even to die when this cannot be attained, and it is remarkable that the same remedy that cures a Swiss, kills a Scot.

Nothing to Say? Say Nothing!
When you have nothing to say, say nothing; a weak defence strengthens your opponent, and silence is less injurious than a bad reply.

Obligations to Many; prudence in repayment
If you are under obligations to many, it is prudent to postpone the recompensing of one, until it be in your power to remunerate all, otherwise you will make more enemies by what you give, than by what you withhold.

Oppressors; their use of declamation
A torrent of declamation, where all is sound and verbiage, has often served the ends of the oppressor, and proved more fatal to the oppressed, than any force of argument or reason that could be brought against him, just as an expert swimmer is in more danger from the froth and foam of the deepest water of the ocean, for although the former has no profundity, it has also no buoyancy, neither can the voice of distress be heard, amidst the roar of the breakers.

Oratory; relic of a semi-barbarous age
Oratory is the huffing and blustering spoilt child of a semi-barbarous age. The Press is the foe of Rhetoric, but the friend of Reason; and the art of declamation has been sinking in value from the moment that speakers were foolish enough to publish and hearers wise enough to read. There are no potentates of modern times that would imitate Phillip, and offer a town of ten thousand inhabitants for an Orator. The ancients were a gossiping and a listening, rather than writing or a reading set....

Our Reputation and Our Life
The two most precious things on this side of the grave are our reputation and our life. But it is to be lamented that the most contemptible whisper may deprive us of the one, and the weakest weapon of the other. A wise man; therefore, will be more anxious to deserve a fair name than to possess it, and this will teach him so to live, as not to be afraid to die.

Passions; strength of

Strong as our passions are, they may be starved into submission, and conquered, without being killed.

Passion vs. Indifference

Matches wherein one party is all passion, and the other all indifference, will assimilate about as well as ice and fire. It is possible that the fire will dissolve the ice, but it is most probable that it will be extinguished in the attempt.

Peace; good vs. bad

A peace, for the making of which, the negotiator has been most liberally rewarded, is usually a bad peace. He is rewarded on the score of having overreached his enemy, and for having made a peace, the advantages of which are clearly on his own side. But such a peace will not be kept; and that is the best peace which is most likely to be the firmest. Now, a peace where the advantages are balanced, and which consults the good of both parties is the firmest because both parties are interested in its preservation, for parchment bonds and seals of state will not restrain a discontented nation, that has arms in her hands, and knows how to use them.

Peace; preserving it is better than a victory

A wise minister would rather preserve peace, than gain a victory; because he knows that, even the most successful war leaves nations generally poorer, always more profligate than it found them. There are real evils that cannot be brought into a list of indemnities, and the demoralizing influence of war is not the least of them. The triumphs of truth are the most glorious, chiefly because they are the most bloodless of all victories, deriving their highest luster, from the number of the *saved,* not of the *slain.*

Pedagogues; their limitations

Man grows up to teach his children as a father, and he looks back to a the time when he himself was taught as a child. Hence he often becomes a pedagogue by circumstance and a dogmatist by choice. He carries these principals beyond his own contracted sphere, into regions without his jurisdiction, and assumes the dignity of the preceptor, in situations where the docility of the pupil would be more consonant to his powers, but less congenial to his pride. Neither are words, those tools he works with, less imperfect than his skill in applying them. Words, *"those fickle daughters of the earth"*, are the creation of a being that is finite, and when applied to explain that which is infinite they fail; for that which is made to surpass not the maker; nor can that which is immeasurable by our thoughts, be measured by our tongues....

Pedantry; effects of

Pedantry crams our heads with learned lumber, and takes out our brains to make room for it.

People; idle vs. industrious

The idle levy a very heavy tax upon the industrious, when by frivolous *visitations* they rob them of their time. Such persons beg their daily happiness from door to door, as beggars their daily bread, and like them, sometimes meet with a rebuff. A mere gossip ought not to wonder if we evince signs that we are tired of him, seeing that we are indebted to the honour of his visit, solely to the circumstances his being tired of himself. He sits at home until he has accumulated an insupportable load of ennui, and he sallies forth to distribute it, amongst all his acquaintances.

Pettifoggers in Law and Empirics in Medicine

Pettifoggers in law and empyrics in medicine, whether their patients lose or save their property or their lives, take care to be, in either case, equally remunerated; they profit by both horns of the dilemma and press defeat, no less than success, into their service. They hold, from time immemorial, the *fee-simple* of a vast estate, subject to no alienation, diminution, revolution, nor tax; all right, title and proprietorship therein; *the folly and ignorance of man-kind.* Over this extensive domain they have long had, by undisputed usage, the sole management and control, in as much as the *real owners* most strenuously and sturdily *disclaim* all right, title and proprietorship therein.

Philosophy vs. Poetry; differences

Philosophy is to Poetry, what old age is to youth; and the stern truths of Philosophy are as fatal to one, as the chilling testimonies of experience are to the hopes of the other.

Physic; most despised by physicians

No men despise physic as much as physicians, because no men so thoroughly understand how little it can perform. They have been tinkering the human constitution four thousand years, in order to cure about as many disorders. The result is that mercury and brimstone are the only two specifics they have discovered. All the fatal maladies continue to be what they were in the days of Paracelsus, Hippocrates and Galen, "*opprobria medicorum*". It is true that each disorder has a thousand prescriptions but not a single remedy. They pour a variety of salts and acids into a marble mortar, and expect similar results when these ingredients are poured into a human stomach; but what can be so groundless as reasoning built on such analogies. It is more safe to imitate the conduct of the late Doctor Heberden; he paid the strictest attention to symptoms, and to temperaments, and having ascertained *these,* to the best of his judgment, he prescribed such remedies as he had always observed to be beneficial to others under *similar* circumstances; and what was of still greater consequences, he carefully avoided all that long experience had taught him would do harm; here he stopped, for he was not so presumptuous as to frame theories to explain the why and the wherefore this did harm and that did good; he was too much occupied in things of greater importance, well knowing that the wisest of us know nothing of life, but *by its effect* and that consequences of every prescription are far more clear and apparent than the causes that produce them.

Pleasing the Mob
It is an easy and a vulgar thing to please the mob, and not a very arduous task to astonish them, but essentially to benefit and to improve them is a work fraught with difficulty, and teeming with danger.

Pleasures: the management of
There is not a little generalship and strategy required in the managing and marshalling of our pleasures, so that each shall not mutually encroach to the destruction of all. For pleasures are very voracious, too apt to worry one another; and each, like Aaron's serpent, is prone to swallow up the rest. Thus drinking will soon destroy the power, gaming the means, and sensuality the taste for other pleasures less seductive but far more salubrious and permanent as they are pure.

Pleasure and Pain; Angels and Devils
If there be a pleasure on earth which angels cannot enjoy, and which they might almost envy man the possession of, it is the power of relieving distress. If there be a pain which devils might pity man for enduring, it is the deathbed reflection that we have possessed the power of doing good but that we have abused and perverted it to purposes of ill.

Politics and Knaves
The first consideration with a knave is how to help himself, and second, how to do it, with an appearance of helping you. Dionysius, the tyrant, stripped the *statue* of Jupiter Olympus, of a robe of massy gold, and substituted a cloak of wool, saying, gold is too cold in winter, and too heavy in summer; — It behooves us *to take care of Jupiter.*

Polylinguists; eloquence is difficult
It is curious that some learned dunces, because they can write nonsense in languages that are dead, should despise those that can speak sense, in languages that are living. To acquire a few tongues, says a French writer, is the task of a few years, but to be eloquent in one, is the labour of a life.

Poor Nations; how to defend
A poor nation that relaxes not from her attitude of defence, is less likely to be attacked, though surrounded by powerful neighbours than another nation which possesses wealth, commerce, population and all the sinews of war, in far great abundance, but *unprepared.* For the more sleek the prey, the greater is the temptation, and no wolf would leave a sheep to dine on a porcupine.

Pope, the; conduct of
The pope conducts himself towards our heavenly master, as a knavish steward does to an earthly one. He says to the tenants, you may continue to neglect my master's interests as much as you please, but keep on good terms with me, and I will take care that you shall be on good terms with my master.

Power; beware of delegation

They that are in power should be extremely cautious to commit the execution of their plans, not only to those who are *able*, but to those who are *willing;* as servants and instrument, it is their duty to do their best, but their employers are never so sure of them, as when their duty is also their *pleasure.* To commit the execution of a purpose, to one who disapproves of the plan of it, is to employ but one *third* of the man; his heart and his head is against you, you have commanded only his hands.

Power; effect of using

Power will intoxicate the best hearts, as wine the strongest heads. No man is wise enough, nor good enough to be trusted with unlimited power; for whatever qualifications he may have evinced to entitle him to the possession of so dangerous a privilege, yet, when possessed, others can no long answer for him, because he can no longer answer for himself.

Powerful vs. Weak; similarities

The worst thing that can be said of the most powerful is, that they can take your life; but the same thing can be said of the most weak.

Praise; Injudicious, effect of

The keenest abuse of our enemies will not hurt as much, in the estimation of the discerning, as the injudicious praise of our friends.

Praise; three kinds

There are three kinds of praise, that which we yield, that which we lend, and that which we pay. We yield it to the powerful from fear, we lend it to the weak from interest, and we pay it to the deserving from gratitude.

Praise of the Envious; not creditable

The praise of the *envious* is far less creditable than their *censure*; they praise only that they can surpass, but that which surpasses them — they censure.

Praise vs. Censure

If men praise your efforts, suspect their judgment; if they censure them, your own.

Praise without Envy; when to expect

Expect not praise without envy until you are dead. Honours bestowed on the illustrious dead, have in them no admixture of envy; for the living pity the dead, and pity and envy, like oil and vinegar assimilate not.

Prayers of Men and God's Will

He that acts toward men as if God saw him, and prays to God, as if men heard him, although he may not obtain all that he asks, or succeed in all that he undertakes, will most probably deserve to do so. For with respect to his actions to men, however he may fail with regard to others, yet *if pure and good* with regard to himself and his highest, they cannot fail; and with respect to his prayers to God, although they cannot make the Deity more *willing* to give, yet they will and must make the supplicant, more *worthy* to receive.

Preachers and Eloquence

The great difficulty in pulpit eloquence is, to give the subject all the dignity it so fully deserves, without attaching any importance to ourselves; some preachers reverse the thing, they give so much importance to themselves, that they have none left for the subject.

Press; parent of good

A free press is the parent of much good in a state. But even a licentious press is a far less evil than a press that is enslaved, because both sides may be heard in the former case, but not in the latter. A licentious press may be an evil; an enslaved press must be so; for an enslaved press may cause error to be more current than wisdom, and wrong more powerful than right; a licentious press cannot affect those things, for if it give the poison; it gives also the antidote, which enslaved press withholds. An enslaved press is doubly fatal, it not only takes away the true light, for in that case we might stand still, but it sets up a false one, that decoys us to our destruction.

Pride; effects of

Pride either finds a desert, or makes one; submission cannot tame its ferocity, nor satiety fill its voracity, and it requires very costly food — its keeper's happiness.

Pride; how to quell it

To quell the pride, even of the greatest, we should reflect how much we owe to others, and how little to ourselves. Phillip having made himself master of Potidoea, received three messengers in one day; the first brought him an account of a great victory, gained over the Illyrians, by his general Parmenio; the second told him, that he was proclaimed victor at the Olympic games; and the third informed him of the birth of Alexander. But there was nothing in all these events that ought to have fed the vanity or that would have justified the pride of Phillip, since, as an elegant writer, Pindar remarks, "for the first he was indebted to his general; for the second, to his horse; and his wife is shrewdly suspected of having helped him to the *third*".

Pride and Ignorance; they are incestuous

It is with nations as with individuals, those who know the least of others think the highest of them; for the whole family of pride and ignorance are incestuous and mutually beget each other. The Chinese affect to despise European ingenuity, but they cannot mend a common watch when it is out of order. They say it is dead and barter it away for a living one.... The Turk will not permit the sacred cities of Mecca or Medina to be polluted by the residence or even footstep of a single Christian; and as to the grand Dairo of Japan, he is so holy, that the sun is not permitted to have the honour of shining on his illustrious head.... Even the pride of Xerxes who fettered the sea; and wrote his commands to Mount Athos, or Caligula, who boasted of an intrigue with the moon, are both surpassed by the petty sovereign of an insignificant tribe in North America, who every morning stalks out of his hovel, bids the sun good morrow, and points out with his finger, the course he is to take for the day... "The Arab" says Zimmerman, "in the conviction that his caliph is infallible, laughs at the stupid credulity of the Tartar, who holds his lama to be immortal".... They also scoff at the superstition of the Tartarian princes who think that their beatification is secure, provided they can eat the holy excrement of the lama.... I have cited these ridiculous extravagancies to show that there are two things in which all sects agree, the hatred with which they pursue the errors of others, and the love with which they cling to their own.

Pride Often Miscalculates

Pride often miscalculates, and more often misconceives. The proud man places himself at a distance from other men; seen from that distance, others perhaps appear little to him; but he forgets that this very distance causes him also to appear equally little to others.

Priests and Physicians; differences

The priest should be careful not to act the reverse of the physician; and in two most important points. The physician renders the most nauseous prescription palatable, by the elegance of its preparation and the winning suavity with which it is recommended; whereas the priest may possibly render a most refreshing cordial disgusting, by the injudicious addition of his own compounds, and the ungracious manner with which they are administered.

Privileges and Immunities; restraints

By privileges, immunities, or prerogatives to give unlimited swing of the passions of individuals, and then to hope that they will restrain them, is about as reasonable as to expect that the tiger will spare the hart, to browse upon the herbage.

Professions; differences between

Of the professions it may be said that soldiers are becoming too popular, parsons too lazy, physicians too mercenary, and lawyers too powerful.

Professors; theories and truth

Professors in every branch of the sciences prefer their own theories to the truth; the reason is, that their theories are *private* property, but truth is *common stock.*

Public Affairs; two remediless and unfortunate evils

In the tortuous and crooked policy of public affairs, as well as in the less extensive, but perhaps more intricate labyrinth of private concerns, there are *two* evils, which must continue to be as remediless as they are unfortunate; they have no cure, and their only palliatives are diffidence and time. They are these — the most candid and enlightened, must give their assent to a probable falsehood, rather than to an improbable truth, and their esteem to those who have a reputation, in preference to those who *only* deserve it.

Quacks of Literature; description
Literature has her quacks no less than medicine, and they are divided into two classes; those who have erudition without genius, and those who have volubility without depth; we shall get second-hand sense from the one, and original nonsense from the other.

Quarrels; prevention of
Two things, well considered, would prevent many quarrels, first, to have it well ascertained whether we are not disputing about terms, rather than things; and, secondly, to examine whether that on which we differ, is worth contending about.

Quarrels; usually fault on both sides
In most quarrels, there is fault on both sides. A quarrel may be compared to a spark, which cannot be produced without a flint, as well as a steel, either of them may hammer on wood forever, no fire will follow.

Rats and Conquerors
Rats and conquerors must expect no mercy in misfortune.

Readers; three types defined
Some read to think — these are rare; some to write, these are common, and some read to talk, and these form the great majority. The first page of an author not infrequently suffices all the purposes of this latter class, of whom it has been said, that they treat books as some do lords; they inform themselves of their *titles,* and then boast of an intimate acquaintance.

Reforms; attempts at
Attempts at reform, when they fail, strengthen despotism, as he that struggles, tightens those cords he does not succeed in breaking.

Refusing a Favour Graciously
There are some who refuse a favour so graciously, as to please us even by the refusal; and there are others who confer an obligation so clumsily, that they please us less by the measure, than they disgust us by the manner of a kindness, as puzzling to our feelings, as the politeness of one, who, if we had dropped our handkerchief, should present it unto us with a pair of tongs!

Relations; take liberties and then refuse help
Relations take the greatest liberties and give the least assistance. If a stranger cannot help us with his purse, he will not insult us with his comments; but with relations, it mostly happens, that they are the veriest misers with regard to their property, but perfect prodigals in the article of advice.

Religion; what men will do for it
Men will wrangle for religion; write for it, fight for it, die for it, any thing but — live for it.

Religion and the False Professors
There only two things in which the false professors of all religions have agreed: to persecute all other sects and to plunder their own.

Religion vs. Knowledge
Religion has treated knowledge sometimes as an enemy, sometimes as a hostage, often as a captive, and more often as a child. But knowledge has become of age; and religion must either renounce her acquaintance, or introduce her as a companion, and respect her as a friend.

Religionists Who Believe Too Much
In all places, and in all times, those Religionists who have believed too much, have been more inclined to violence and persecution, than those who have believed too

little. I suspect the reason is that indifference is a much less active principle than enthusiasm.

Religions; true and false
Where true religion has prevented one crime, false religions have afforded a pretext for a thousand.

Repartee; when it is perfect
Repartee is perfect, when it effects its purpose with a double edge. Repartee is the highest order of wit, as it bespeaks the coolest yet quickest exercise of genius, at a moment when the passions are aroused. Voltaire on hearing the name of Haller mentioned to him by an English traveller at Ferney, burst forth in a violent panegyric upon him. His visitor told that such praise was most disinterested, or that Haller by no means spoke so highly of him. "Well, well, *n'importe*", replied Voltaire, "perhaps we were *both* mistaken".

Repentance; the seeds of
The seeds of repentance are sown in youth by pleasure, but the harvest is reaped in age by pain.

Reputation; how acquired
There are two modes of establishing our reputation; to be praised by honest men and, to be abused by rogues. It is best, however, to secure the former, because it will be invariably accompanied by the latter. His calumniation is not only the greatest benefit a rogue can confer upon us, but it is also the only service that he will perform for nothing.

Restorations; where did all the heroes come from?
At the restoration of Charles the Second the tide of opinion set so strong in favour of loyalty, that the principal annalist of that day pauses to express his wonder where all the men came from, who had done all the mischief; but this was the surprise of ignorance; for it is in politics, as in religion, that none run into such extremes as renegades, or so ridiculously overact their parts. The passions on those occasions take their full swing and react like the pendulum, whose oscillations on one side, will always be regulated by the height of the arc it has subtended on the other.

Retirement and Acts of Magnanimity
In the obscurity of retirement, in the squalid poverty and revolting privations of a cottage, it has often been my lot to witness scenes of magnanimity and self denial, as much beyond the belief, as the practice of the great; an heroism borrowing no support, either from the gaze of the many, or the admiration of the few, yet, flourishing amidst ruins, and on the confines of the grave; a spectacle as stupendous in the moral world, as the falls of the Missouri in the natural and, like that mighty cataract, doomed to display its grandeur, only where there are no eyes to appreciate its magnificence.

Revenge; blood letting is not a remedy
Revenge is a fever in our own blood, to be cured only by letting the blood of another; but the remedy too often produces a relapse; which is remorse — a malady far more dreadful than the first disease, because it is incurable.

Revenge vs. Forgiveness; differences
The sun should not set upon our anger; neither should it rise upon our confidence. We should forgive freely, but forget rarely. I will not be revenged, and this I owe to my enemy, but I will remember, and this I owe to myself.

Revenge vs. Malice; when all the world are knaves
It proceeds rather from revenge than malice, when we hear a man affirms, that all the world are knaves. For before a man draws this conclusion of the world, the world has usually anticipated him, and concluded all this of him who makes the observation. Such men may be compared to Brothers the *prophet* who, on being asked by a friend how he came to be clapped up into Bedlam, replied, "I and the world happened to have a slight difference of opinion. The world said I was mad, and I said the world was mad; I was *outvoted*, and here I am."

Revolutions; failure of the demagogues
It is far easier to pull down, than to build up and to destroy, than to preserve. Revolutions have on this account been falsely supposed to be fertile of great talent; as the dregs rise to the top, during fermentation, and the lightest things are carried highest by the whirlwind. And the practice of this proposition bears out the theory; for demagogues have succeeded tolerably well in making ruins; but the moment they begin to build anew from the materials they have overthrown, they have often been uselessly employed with regard to others, and more often dangerously with regard to themselves. "*Fracta compage ruebant.*"*
* "The bands being broken, the structure falls."

Rich; their impotence when ill
It is only when the rich are sick, that they fully feel the impotence of wealth.

Rich Patients and Poor Physicians
The rich patient cures the poor physician much more often than the poor physician the rich patient; and it is rather paradoxical that the rapid recovery of the one, usually depends upon the procrastinated disorder of the other. Some persons will tell you, with an air of the miraculous, that they recovered *although* they were given over, whereas they might with more reason have said, they recovered *because* they were given over.

Riches; are easy to hide
If rich, it is easy enough to conceal our wealth; but, if poor, it is not quite so easy to conceal our poverty. We shall find that it is less difficult to hide a thousand guineas, than one hole in our coat.

Riches and Preferment
Many speak the truth, when they say they despise riches and preferment, but they mean the riches and preferment possessed by *other men.*

Rich Men; one privilege they enjoy
The greatest and the most amiable privilege which the rich enjoy over the poor, is that which they exercise the least — the privilege of making them happy.

Rights; deprivation of, effects
A system of mal-government begins by refusing man his rights, and ends by depriving him of the power of appreciating the value of that which he has lost. It is possible that a Polish serf, or the Russian boor, or the descendant of the kidnapped Negro, may be contented with their condition; but it is not possible that the mind of a Franklin, or a Howard, could be contented to see them so. The philosopher knows that the most degrading symptom of hopeless vassalage is this very apathy that it super induces on its victims, as the surgeon knows that the most alarming symptom of a deadly mortification having taken place is the cessation of pain on the part of the patient.

Road to Heaven is Through Hell
It would be very unfortunate if there was no other road to Heaven, but through Hell yet this dangerous and impractical road has been attempted by all these princes, potentates and statesmen, who have done evil, in order that good may come.

Roman Conduct against Christians
When we apply to the conduct of the ancient Romans, the pure and unbending principles of Christianity, we try those noble delinquents unjustly, in as much as we condemn them by the severe sentence of an *"ex post facto"* law.

Royal Favourites; their obligations to their masters
Royal favourites are often obliged to carry their complaisance farther then they meant. They live for their master's pleasure, and they die for his convenience.

Russia Defending Itself
Russia like the elephant, is rather unwieldy in attacking others, but most formidable in defending itself. She proposes this dilemma to all invaders, — a dilemma that Napoleon discovered too late. The horns of it are short and simple, but strong *"Come to me with few, and I will overwhelm you; come to me with many, and you shall overwhelm yourselves"*.

Safety; that bought by power is unsafe
A man may arrive at such power, and be so successful in the application of it, as to be enabled to crush and to overwhelm all his enemies. But a safety built upon successful vengeance, and established not upon our love, but upon our fear, often contains within itself the seeds of its own destruction. It is at best a joyless and a precarious safety, as short-lived as that of some conquerors, who have died from a pestilence, excited by the dead bodies of the vanquished.

Saints and Sinners; intolerance of those saved
No roads are so rough as those that have just been mended, so no sinners are so intolerant as those that have just turned saints.

Saints and Sinners; who's who
Some *reputed* saints that have been canonized, ought to have been cannonaded, and some *reputed* sinners that have been cannonaded, ought to have been canonized.

Scriptures; as aid to potentates
There is one passage in the Scriptures to which all of the potentates of Europe seem to have given their unanimous consent and approbation, and to have studied so thoroughly as to have it quite at their fingers' ends *"There went out a decree in the days of Claudius Cesar that all the world should be taxed"*.

Secrecy; the soul of all great designs
Secrecy has been well termed the soul of all great designs; perhaps more has been effected by concealing our own intentions, than by discovering those of the enemy. But great men succeed in both.

Secrets; who are the fondest of them?
None are as fond of secrets as those who do not mean to keep them; such persons covet secrets, as a spend-thrift covets money; for the purpose of circulation.

Shakespeare *et al.*
Shakespeare, Butler and Bacon, have rendered it extremely difficult for all who come after them, to be sublime, witty, or profound.

Shakespeare Stands Alone
All the poets are indebted more or less to those who have gone before them, even Homer's originality has been questioned, and Virgil owes almost as much to Theocritus in his Pastorals, as to Homer in his Heroics ... but Shakespeare stands alone. His want of erudition was a most happy and productive ignorance; it forced him back upon his own resources, which were exhaustless. If his literary qualifications made it impossible for him to borrow from the ancients, he was more than repaid by the powers of his invention, which made borrowing unnecessary. In all the ebbings and flowings of his genius, in his storms, no less than in his calms, he is as completely separated from all other poets, as the Caspian from all other seas.

But he abounds with so many axioms applicable to all the circumstances, situations, and varieties of life that they are no longer the property of the poet, but of the world; all apply, but none dare appropriate them; and, like anchors, they are secure from thieves, by reason of their weight.

Singing; a dangerous gift

He that can charm a whole company by singing, and at the age of thirty has no cause to regret the possession of so dangerous a gift, is a very extraordinary, and, I may add, a very fortunate man.

Singularity; how to achieve it

Let those who would affect singularity with success, first determine to be very virtuous, and they will soon be sure to be very singular.

Slander; effects of

Slander cannot make the subjects of it either better or worse, it may represent us in a false light, or place a likeness of us in a bad one, but we are the same; not so the slanderer; for calumny always make the calumniator worse, but the calumniated – never.

Sleep; a type of death

Sleep, a type of death, is also, like that which it typified, restricted to the earth. It flies from hell, and is excluded from heaven.

Society; must be viewed in all situations

Society like a shaded silk must be viewed in all situations, or its colours will deceive us.... The philosopher, therefore, will draw his estimate of human nature, by varying as much as possible his own situation, to multiply the points of view under which he observes her.... He will also associate with the highest, without servility, and with the lowest, without vulgarity. In short, in the grand theatre of human life, he will visit the pit and the gallery, as well as the boxes, but he will not inform the boxes that he comes amongst them from the pit, nor the pit that he visits them from the gallery.

Soldiers; reasons for fighting

An Irishman fights before he reasons, a Scotchman reasons before he fights, an Englishman is not particular to the order of precedence, but will do either to accommodate his customers. A modern general has said that the best troops would be as follows: An Irishman half drunk, a Scotchman half starved, and an Englishman with his belly full.

Sowing the Wind, Reaping the Whirlwind

If those alone who *"sowed the wind, did reap the whirlwind,"* it would be well. But the mischief is, that the blindness of bigotry, the madness of ambition, and the miscalculation of diplomacy, seek their victims principally amongst the innocent and the unoffending. The cottage is sure to suffer for every error of the court, the cabinet or the camp. When error sits in the seat of power and of authority, and is generated in high places, it may be compared to that torrent which originates indeed in the mountains, but commits its devastation in the vale.

Statesman; his pay and why
It is curious that we pay statesmen for what they say, not for what they do; and judge of them from what they do, not from what they say. Hence they have one code of maxims for profession, and another for practice, and make up their consciences, as the Neapolitans do their beds, with one set of furniture for show, and another for use.

Style; ease in style
Nothing is so difficult as the apparent case of a clear and flowing style; those graces which, from their presumed facility, encourage all to attempt an imitation of them, are usually the most inimitable.

Subtlety; sometimes give safety
Subtlety will sometimes give safety, no less than strength, and minuteness has sometimes escaped, where magnitude would have been crushed. The little animal that kills the Boa, is formidable chiefly from its insignificance, which is incompressible by the folds of its antagonist.

Suicide; not always from cowardice
Suicide sometimes proceeds from cowardice, but not always; for cowardice sometimes prevents it; since as many live because they are afraid to die, as die because they are afraid to live.

Talent vs. Inferior Minds
It is adverse to talent, to be consorted and trained with inferior minds, or inferior companions, *however high they may rank.* The foal of a racer, neither finds out his speed, nor calls out his powers, if pastured out with the common herd, that are destined for the collar, and the yoke.

Testimony of Those Who Doubt the Least
The testimony of those who doubt the least is not, unusually, that very testimony that ought to be most doubted.

Three Professions; how they can save themselves trouble
There are three things that, well understood, and conscientiously practiced, would save the three professions a vast deal of trouble; but we must not expect that every member of the three professions would thank us for such a discovery, for some of them have too much time on their hands; and a philosopher would be more inclined to smile than to wonder, should he now and then hear a physician crying down, *regimen,* a lawyer, *equity,* or a priest, *morality.*

Travel; the effects of
That knowledge, which a man may acquire *only* by travelling, is often too dearly bought. The traveler indeed may be said to fetch the knowledge, as the merchant his wares, to be enjoyed and applied, by those who stay home. A man may sit by his own fireside, be conversant with many domestic arts and general sciences, and yet have very correct ideas of the manners, habits and customs of *other* nations. While on the contrary, he that has spent his whole life in travelling ... and, has made his *legs his compasses,* may live and die a thorough novice in all the most important concerns of life ... and he may have been round the world, and over the world, without having been *in* the world; and die an ignoramus, even after having performed the seven journeys between the holy hills; swept the Kaaba with a silver besom, drank of the holy waters of the Zemzem; and traced the source of the Nile, and the end of the Niger.

True Friendship; its value
True friendship is like sound health, the value of it is seldom known until it is lost.

Trumping the King
King James held convocation at Perth, and demanded of the Scotch barons that they should produce the charters by which they held their lands; they all with one simultaneous movement, rose up and drew their swords.

Trust; kinds of
We generally covet that particular trust which we are least likely to keep. He that thoroughly knows his friends, might, perhaps with safety, confide his wife to the care of one, his purse to another, and his secrets to a third, when to permit them to make their own choices would be his ruin.

Truth; more or less, effect of
There are many who say more than the truth on some occasions, and balance the account with their conscience, by saying less than the truth on others. But the fact is, that they are, in both instances, as fraudulent, as he would be, that exacted more from *his* due from his debtors, and paid less than *their* due to his creditors.

Vengeance; a dangerous tool

A man may arrive at such power, and be so successful in the application of it, as to be enabled to crush and to overwhelm all his enemies. But a safety, built upon successful vengeance, and established not upon our love, but upon fear, often contains within itself the seeds of its own destruction. It is at best joyless and a precarious safety, as short-lived as that of some conquerors, who have died from a pestilence, excited by the dead bodies of the vanquished.

Vice, Virtue and Time

He that is good will infallibly become better, and he that is bad will as certainly become worse: for vice, virtue and time are three things that never stand still.

Vices, Private; do not cause public benefits

The policy of drawing a public revenue from the private vices of drinking, and of gambling, is as purblind as it is pernicious; for temperate men drink the most, because they drink the longest; and a gamester contributes much less to the revenue than the industrious, because he is much sooner ruined. When Mandeville maintained that private vices were public benefits he did not calculate the widely destructive influence of bad example. To affirm that a vicious man is only his *own* enemy, is about as wise as to affirm that a virtuous man is only his *own* friend.

Vicious vs. Virtuous; their sufferings and rewards

The horrible catastrophes that sometimes happen to the vicious are as salutary to others by their warning, as the most brilliant rewards of the virtuous are, by their example. And on the contrary the successes of the bad, and the sufferings of the good, might make us tremble for the interests of virtue, were not these things the strongest proofs of a hereafter.

Villains are the worst casuists

Villains are usually the worst casuists, and rush into greater crimes to avoid less. Henry the eighth committed murder to avoid the imputation of adultery; and in our times, those who commit the latter crime attempt to wash off the stain of seducing the wife, by signifying their readiness to *shoot* the *husband!*

Virtue; tax which must be paid

This is the tax a man must pay to his virtues, — they hold up a torch to his vices, and render those frailties notorious in him which would have passed without observation in another.

Virtue; the pursuit of

There is but *one* pursuit in life which it is in the power of all to follow, and of all to attain. It is subject to no disappointments, since he that perseveres, makes every difficulty an advancement and every contest a victory; and this is the pursuit of virtue. Sincerely to aspire after virtue, is to gain her, and zealously to labour after her wages, is to receive them. Those that seek her early, will find her before it is late; her reward also is with her, and she will come quickly. For the breast of a good man is a little heaven commencing on earth; where the Deity sits enthroned with unrivalled influence, every subjugated passion, "like the wind and storm, fulfilling his word".

Virtue without Talent; defined
Virtue without talent, is a coat of *mail,* without a *sword;* it may indeed defend the wearer, but will not enable him to protect his friend.

War; a game few win
War is a game in which princes seldom win; the people never. To be *defended* is almost as great an evil as to be attacked; and the peasant has often found the shield of a protector an instrument not less oppressive than the sword of an invader. Wars of opinion, as they have been the most destructive, are also the most disgraceful of conflicts; being appeals from right to might, and from argument to artillery. The fomenters of them have considered the *raw material* man, to have been formed for no worthier purposes than to fill up gazettes at home, with their names, and ditches abroad with their bodies. But let us hope that true philosophy, the joint offspring of a religion that is pure, and of a reason that is enlightened, will gradually prepare a better order of things, when mankind will no longer be insulted by seeing bad pens mended by good swords, and weak heads exalted by strong hands.

War and Peace; with the first, parsimony, with the second, prodigality
As in public life, that minister that makes war with parsimony must make peace with prodigality. So in private life, those hostile but feeble measures which only serve to irritate our enemies, not to intimidate them, are by all means to be avoided; for he that has recourse to them, only imposes on himself the ultimate necessity of purchasing reconciliation often expensive, always humiliating.

Wars: effect on the body politic
Wars are to the body politic, what drams are to the individual, there are times when they may prevent a sudden death, but if frequently resorted to, or long persisted in, they heighten the energies, only to hasten the dissolution.

Wealth; what is enough?
Agar said, "Give me neither poverty nor riches, and this will ever be the prayer of the wise" Our incomes should be like our shoes, if too small, they will gall and pinch us, but, if too large, they will cause us to stumble, and to trip. But wealth, after all, is a relative thing, since he that has little, and wants less, is richer than he that has much, but wants more. True contentment depends not upon what we would have; a tub was large enough for Diogenes, but a world was too little for Alexander.

Wealth is a Snare
Our wealth is often a snare to ourselves, and *always* a temptation to others.

Wealth vs. Talent
Gross and vulgar minds will always pay higher respect to wealth than to talent, for wealth, although, it be a far less efficient source of power than talent, happens to be far more intelligible.

When the Million Applaud You
When the million applaud you, seriously ask yourself what harm you have done; when they censure you, what good!

Wisdom; be slow to believe you have it
Be very slow to believe that you are wiser than all others; it is a fatal but common error. Where one has been saved by a true estimation of another's weakness, thousands have been destroyed by a false appreciation of their own strength. Napoleon could calculate the *former* well, but to his miscalculation of the *latter*, he may ascribe his present degradation.

Wit; defined
There is no quality of the mind, nor of the body, that so instantaneously and irresistibly captivates, as wit. An elegant writer has observed that wit may do very well for a mistress, but that he should prefer reason for a wife. He that deserts the latter, and gives himself up entirely to the guidance of the former will certainly fall into many pitfalls and quagmires, like him, who walks by flashes of lightning, rather than by the steady beams of the sun.

Wit Is Not Difficult
It is not difficult to fill a comedy with good repartee, as might be at first imagined, if we consider how completely *both* parties are in the power of the author. The blaze of wit in the School for Scandal astonishes us less when we remember that the writer had it in his power to frame both the question and the answer; the reply and the rejoinder; the time and the place. He must be a poor proficient, who cannot keep up the game, when the ball, the wall, and the racket are at his *sole* command.

Wit in Women
It has been said, that to excel them in wit, is a thing the men find is the most difficult to pardon in the women. This feeling, if it produces only emulation, is right, if envy, it is wrong. For a high degree of intellectual refinement in the female, is the surest pledge society can have for the improvement of the male. But wit in women is a jewel, which, unlike all others, borrows luster *from* its setting, rather than bestows it; since nothing is so easy to fancy a very beautiful woman extremely witty. Even Madame de Stael admits that she discovered, that as she grew old, the men could not find out that wit in her at fifty, which she possessed at twenty-five; and yet the external attractions of this lady were by no means equal to those of her mind.

Wits Who Pervert Their Talents
Great wits, who pervert their talents to sap the foundation of morality, have to answer for all the evils that lesser wits may accomplish through their means, even to the end of time. A heavy load of responsibility, where the mind is still alive to do mischief, when the hand it animated is dust. Men of talent may make a breach in morality, at which men of none may enter, as a citadel may be carried by muskets, after a road has been battered out for them by cannon.

Women; dangerous when slighted
Most females will forgive a liberty, rather than a slight, and if any woman were to hang a man for stealing her picture, although it were set in gold, it would be a new

case in law; but, if he carried off the setting and left the portrait, I would not answer for his safety, even if Alley were his pleader, and a Middlesex jury his peers. The felon would be doomed to feel experimentally, the force of two lines of the poet, which, on this occasion, I shall unite: *"Foemina quid possit, spretaquae injuria formae"**.
* "What things a woman when despised can do."

Women; how a plain man wins them
The plainest man who pays attention to women will sometimes succeed as well as the handsomest man who does not. Wilkes observed to Lord Townsend, "You, my lord, are the handsomest man in the kingdom, and I the plainest. But I would give your lordship half an hour's start, and yet come up with you in the affections of any woman we both wished to win; because all those attentions which you would omit on the score of your fine exterior, I should be obliged to pay, owing to the deficiencies in mine".

Women: pretensions to virtue vs. approbation of men
It is far more safe to lower any pretensions that a woman may aspire to, on the score of her virtue, than those *dearer* ones which she may foster on the side of her vanity. Tell her that she is not in the exact road to gain the approbation of angels, and she may not only hear you with patience, but may even follow your advice, but should you venture to hint to her, that she is equally unsuccessful in all her methods to gain the approbation of *men,* and she will pursue not the advice, but the adviser, certainly with scorn, probably with vengeance.

Women; the pleasure of their company
We seek the society of the ladies with a view to be pleased, rather than to be instructed, and are more gratified by those who will talk, than by those that are silent; for if they talk well, we are doubly delighted to receive information from so pleasant a source, and if they are at times a little out in their conclusions, it is flattering to our vanity, to set them right. Therefore I would have the ladies indulge with somewhat less of reserve in the freedom of conversation, if notwithstanding the remark of him who said with more of point than politeness, that they were the very reverse of their own mirrors, for the one reflected, without talking, but the other talked without reflecting.

Women and Pleasure; described
Pleasure is to women what the sun is to the flower; if moderately enjoyed, it beautifies, it refreshes, and it improves; if immoderately, it withers, etiolates, and destroys. But the duties of domestic life, exercised as they must be in retirement, and calling forth all the sensibilities of the female, are perhaps as necessary to the full development of her charms, as the shade and shower are to the rose, confirming its beauty, and increasing its fragrance.

Women of Fashion
Ladies of Fashion starve their happiness to feed their vanity, and their love to feed their pride.

Women of the East; personal charms vs. intellectual powers
In the East, the women are chosen with reference to their personal charms, rather than their intellectual, considered as ministers to sensuality, rather than as ornaments of Society, and abandoned the moment the slightest decay begins to manifest itself in those corporeal attractions which first enhanced their value, and ensured their admiration. It would seem that there is a sound physical cause for this low and animal mode of appreciating female excellence, so prevalent in the East, and in calculating which, if compared with the northern nations, the body has so much more weight in the scale, than the mind. The fact is, that under the ripening suns of the East, all the charms and beauties are developed, long before the less precocious mind has put forth even the promise and the blossom of its ultimate but progressive perfection. But inasmuch as premature adolescence, the charms of the body has a constant tendency to super induce premature decrepitude, the charms of the body have ceased to flourish, when those of the mind are beginning to expand and to bud. Thus the unfortunate pride of the Harem has ceased to please as the mistress precisely at the moment when she might begin to interest as the friend.

World; how to explain its difficulties
This world cannot explain its own difficulties, without the assistance of another.

Youth; excesses of
The excesses of our youth are drafts upon our age payable with interest, about thirty years
after date.

Youth and Old Age; differences in
Let us so employ our youth that the very old age, which will deprive us of attention from the eyes of the woman shall enable to replace what we have lost with something better, from the ears of the men.

The Recycle Bin

(Editor's Note)

Working my way through "*Lacon*" (there were 451 pages of small type in the 1826 edition) looking for aphorisms which I thought might be of interest to the reader, I kept unearthing odds and ends of information I found entertaining. Some were in the form of footnotes, many were anecdotal asides of the author (Colton liked anecdotes) and some were buried deep in the almost impenetrable prose of multi-paged essays on arcane subjects. I decided to collect these and include them with the aphorisms. They present a smorgasbord of items, characters and subjects which do not deserve to be buried for another 180 years, so I recycled them.

G.J.B.

Index

Recycle Bin

Actors and the Art of Acting

Histrionic talent is not so rare a gift as some imagine, it is both overrated and over paid. That the requisites for a first rate actor demand a combination not easily to be found, is an erroneous assumption, ascribable, perhaps, to the following causes. The market for this kind of talent must always be *under stocked*, because very few of those who are really qualified to gain theatrical fame, will condescend to start for it. To succeed, the candidate must be a gentleman by nature, and a scholar by education. There are many who can justly boast of this union, but out of that many, how few there are that would seek or desire theatrical celebrity. The metropolitan theatre, therefore, can only be recruited from the best samples which the provincial theatres will afford, and this is a market, abundant as to quantity, but extremely deficient as to quality....

In general, those who possess the necessary qualifications for an actor, also feel that they deserve to be something better, and this feeling dictates a more respectable arena. Neither is the title to talent bestowed by the suffrages of a metropolitan audience, always unequivocal. Such an audience is, indeed, a tribunal from which an actor has no appeal; but there are many causes which conspire to warp and bias its judgment; and it often happens that it is more difficult to *please a country audience,* than a London one.

In a country theatre there is nothing to bribe our decisions; the principal actor is badly supported and must depend solely on himself. In a London Theatre, the blaze of lights and beauty, the splendour of the scenery, the skill of the orchestra, are all adscititious* attractions, acting as *avant* couriers for the performer, and predisposing us be pleased. Add to this, that the extended magnificence of a metropolitan stage defends the actor from that microscopic scrutiny to which he must submit in the country.

We should also remember that at times it requires more courage to praise than to censure, and the metropolitan actor will always have *this* advantage over the provincial, if we are pleased, our taste is flattered in the one instance, suspected in the other.
* "adscititious" – assumed, adopted from without, supplemented. Oxford Shorter English Dictionary, 3rd edition.

Antiquity; a nation's pride in it is misplaced

It is with antiquity as with ancestry, nations are proud of the one, and individuals of the other, but if they are nothing in themselves, that which is their pride ought to be their humiliation. If an individual is worthy of his ancestors, why extol those with whom he is on a level, and if he is unworthy of them, to laud them, is to libel himself.

And, nations also, when they boast of their antiquity,* only tell us in other words, that they are standing on the ruins of so many generations. But if their view of things is limited, and their prospect of the sciences narrow and confined, if other nations who stand upon no such eminence, see farther than they do, is not the very antiquity of which they boast, a proof that their forefathers were not giants in knowledge, or if they were, that their children have degenerated. The Babylonians laid claim to an antiquity of four hundred and seventy thousand years, founded on a series of astronomical observations. But with all their knowledge of the heavens, they knew no more of things appertaining to the earth, than their neighbours, and they suffered their glory to be eclipsed, by a little horde of Macedonians.

The Chinese of the present day are not behind, in hand with the Babylonians in looking backwards, but with most other nations in looking forwards. They unite all the presumption with all the prejudice of ignorance. As a nation, notwithstanding their longevity, they have not yet arrived at manhood, and when they boast of their antiquity, they openly boast of a more protracted period of childhood and imbecility.

*I do not mean to deny the probability that a state of society highly cultivated and refined, may have existed in various parts of the globe, previous to any written or authentic documents that have been transmitted to us. India is not without monuments of such a state of civilization, and some late discoveries go to establish the same supposition even in America. I admit that it is fairer to infer such a state of things from monuments that are extant, than to assert its non-existence from the want of documents which after all may have been left, but may also have been lost.

Setting aside the traditions of the Athenians, concerning their Musaeus, of the Thebans of their Linus, of the Thracians as regards their Orpheus, or the Phoenicians of Cadmus, yet still it must be admitted that Thales did actually discover a state of society in the East, which would have justified him on his return from travelling, in applying the same degrading title to the Greeks themselves, which they afterwards bestowed upon others. The magnificent ruins of ancient cities, of which no record remains, the pyramids, concerning which the remotest antiquity has nothing to depose, the advanced state of the science of geometry and astronomy amongst the Egyptians and the Babylonians do warrant us of after times, in the presumption that a high state of cultivation and knowledge did exist anterior to any written documents, or historical records; but after all, both individuals and nations, when they vaunt themselves on what they *were*, must do it at the hazard of provoking enquiry as to what they *are*.

But it ought to suppress the arrogance of national talent to reflect, that destruction may have caused many things to be discoveries, which without it, to us at least, had been none; and a pride founded only on antiquity, may also be rebuked, in a nation that suffers more modern ones to outstrip it, on the principle that they have made so bad a use of so long an experience, and have profited so little, in having neither been taught by the wisdom, nor warned by the folly of their forefathers.

Authors of Talent and Genius; their viewpoint of the mob

An author of talent and genius, must not hope that the plodding manufacturers of dullness will admire him, it is expecting too much, they cannot admire him without first despising themselves When I look out of my window, and see what a motley mob it is, high and low, mounted and pedestrian, that an author is ambitious to please, I am ashamed of myself, for feeling the slightest anxiety, as to the verdict of such a tribunal. When I leave this class of judges, for that which aspires to be more intellectual, I then indeed feel somewhat more ground for anxiety, but less for hope; for in this court I find that my judges have their claims and pretensions no less than myself, pretensions that are neither so low as to be despised, nor so high as to be above all danger of suffering by competition. So small indeed is the fountain of fame, and so numerous the applicants, that it is often rendered turbid, by the struggles of those very claimants who have the least chance of partaking of the stream, but whose thirst is not at all diminished, by any sense of their unworthiness.

Blood, circulation of, I

Andrew Caesalphinus, chief physician to Pope Clement VIII, published a book at Pisa on the 1st of June, 1569, entitled "Questionum Peripateticarum, Libri V" in which there is this passage, which evidently shows that he was thoroughly acquainted with the circulation of blood: "Idcirco Pulmo per venam arteriis similem, ex dextro cordis ventriculo, fervidum, harries sanguinem eumque per anastamosim arteriae venali reddens quae in sinistrum cordia ventriculum tendit, transmisso interim aere frigido per aspere arterie canales, quid juxta arterium venalem protenduntur non tamen osculis communicantes, ut putavit Galenus solo tactu temperat. Huic sanguinis circulationi ex dextro cordis ventriculo, pur pulmones in sinistrum ejusdem ventriculum, optime respondent ca quae ex dissectione apparent. Nam duo sunt vasa in dextrum ventriculum desinentia, duo etiam in sinistrum.duorum autem, unum intromittit tantum alterum educit membranus eo ingenio compositia."

Blood; circulation of, II

"Harvey, William. Born 1578, died 1657. English physician, discoverer of the circulation of the blood. Educated at Cambridge, and then proceeded to Padua, Italy to study medicine under H. Fabricius and became doctor of medicine in 1602. He returned to England and in 1607 was admitted to the Royal College of Physicians as a fellow. In 1609 he obtained the post of physician to St. Bartholomew's Hospital. In 1616 he began a course of lectures at the College of Physicians in which he first brought forward his views on the movements of the heart and blood.

In 1628 he published the *"excercitatio anatomica de motu cordis et sanguinis* ('Anatomical exercise and motions of the heart and blood')" *Encyclopedia Britannica, 1955 ed.*

Blood; practice of vaccination

As I have a remark on inoculation in the article to which this note refers, I shall quote an ingenious writer, who says, "When it was observed that the inoculation produced fewer pustules and did not disfigure the countenance like the natural smallpox, the practice was immediately adopted in those countries, where the beauty of the females constituted an important source of wealth, as for example in Georgia and Circassia." "The Indians and the Chinese," says the same writer, "have practiced inoculation for many ages, in all the empire of the Burmahs, in the island of Ceylon, in Siam and in Cambodia." Vol. I, Article 352.

Brass wheels and George Washington

In the complicated and marvellous machinery of circumstances it is almost impossible to decide what would have happened, as to some events, if the slightest disturbance had taken place, in the march of those that *preceded* them.

We may observe a little dirty wheel of brass, spinning round upon its greasy axle, and the result is, that in another apartment, many yards distance from it, a beautiful piece of silk issues from a loom, rivaling in its hues the tints of the rainbow; there are myriads of events in our lives, the distance between which was much greater than that between this wheel and ribbon, but where the connection has been much more close.

If a private country gentleman in Cheshire, about the year 17 hundred and thirty* had not been overturned in his carriage, it is extremely probable that America, instead of being a free republic at this moment, would have continued a dependent colony of England. This country gentleman happened to be Augustus Washington, Esquire, who was thus accidentally thrown *into* the company of a lady who afterwards became his wife, who emigrated with him to America, and in the year 17 hundred and thirty-two, at Virginia, became the envied mother of George Washington, the great.
"George Washington was born on Feb 22 (old style) Feb 11, 1732 at Bridges' Creek, Virginia", Encyclopedia Brittanica, 1953 edition.

Civil Law Suits; a luxury?

Jeremy Bentham considers litigation a great evil and deems it the height of cruelty to load a law-suit, which is one evil, with taxation, which is another. It would be quite as fair, he thinks, to tax a man for being ill, by enacting that no physician should write a prescription without a stamp. Mr. Pitt, on the contrary, considered *a law-suit a luxury!* And held that, like other luxuries, it ought to be taxed, "Westminster Hall" said he, "is as open to any man as the London Tavern". To which Mr. Sheridan replied, "he that entered either without money, would meet with a very scurvy reception".

Some will say that the heavy expense of law prevents the frequency of law-suits, but the practice does not confirm the theory. Others will say that they originate from men of obstinate and quarrelsome dispositions, and that such ought to suffer from their folly. There would be something in this, provided it was not necessary for a wise man to take a shield, when a fool has taken a sword.

Law-suits, indeed, do generally originate with the obstinate and the ignorant, but they do not end with them, and that lawyer was right who left all his money to the support of an asylum for fools and lunatics, saying that from such he got it, and to such he would bequeath it.

Oratory; the art of

An orator, who, like Demosthenes, appeals to the head, rather than the heart, who resorts to argument, not to sophistry, who has no sounding words, unsupported by strong conceptions, who would rather convince without persuading, than persuade without convincing, is an exception to all rules, and would succeed in all periods. When the Roman people had listened to the long, diffuse and polished discourses of Cicero, they departed, saying to one another, what a splendid speech our orator has made, but when the Athenians heard Demosthenes, he so filled them with the subject matter of his oration, that they quite forgot the orator, but left him at the finish of his harangue, breathing revenge, and exclaiming, let us go and fight against Phillip.

Princes; are also aware that all politics are local

Princes rule the people, and their passions rule princes; but Providence can overrule the whole, and draw the instruments of his inscrutable purposes from the vices, no less than from the virtues of kings. Thus the Reformation, which was planted by the lust of Henry the Eighth of England, was preserved by the ambition of Philip the Second of Spain.

Queen Mary would have sacrificed Elizabeth to the full establishing of the Catholic faith, if she had not been prevented by Philip the Second, her husband, who foresaw, in the death of Elizabeth, the succession of Mary Stewart, who was then married to Francis the Second; and in that succession, he anticipated the certain union of Great Britain and France; an event that would have dispersed to the winds his own ambitious dream of universal monarchy. The consequences were, the life of Elizabeth was preserved, and the Protestant cause prevailed.

Science; dotage or infancy?

It has been asked whether we are in the dotage, or infancy of science; a question that involves its own answer; not in the infancy, because we have learnt much; not in the dotage, because we have much to learn.

The fact is, we are in a highly progressive state of improvement, and it astonishing, in how geometrical a ratio the march of knowledge proceeds. Each new discovery affords fresh light to guide us to the exploration of another, until all the dark corners of our ignorance be visited by the rays. Things apparently obscure, have ultimately illustrated even those that are obvious; thus the alchemist in his very failures has enlightened the chemist; and the visionary astrologer, though consistently false in his prophecies as to those little events going on upon the earth, has enabled the astronomer truly to predict those great events that are taking place in the heavens.

Thus it is that one experiment diffuses its sparks for the examination of a second, each assisting each, and all the whole. Discussion and investigation are gradually accomplishing that for the intellectual light, which refraction and reflection have ever done for the solar, and it is now neither hopeless nor extravagant to anticipate that glorious era when truth herself shall have climbed the zenith of her meridian, and shall refresh the nations with her *"Day Springs from on high"*.

Science; the state of medical knowledge in the early 19th century

The Chinese, who aspire to be thought an enlightened nation, to this day are ignorant of the circulation of the blood; and even in England, the man who made that noble discovery, lost all his practice in consequence of his ingenuity, and Hume informs us, that no physician in the united kingdoms who has attained the age of forty, ever submitted to become a convert to Harvey's theory, but went on preferring *mumpsimus* to *symposiums** to the day of his death. So true is that line of the satyrist *"a fool at forty, is a fool indeed"* and may we add another line from another satyrist: *"Durum est, Quae juvenes didicere; senes perdenda futeri"***.

* An incorrect, but popular expression taking the place of a correct one

** "It is hard to think that worthless, which, as boys they have toiled to learn"

Statesmen; regulated by secret springs and causes

Some historians, like Tacitus, Burnmet, and the Abbe Raynal, are never satisfied, without adding to their detail of events, the secret springs and causes that have produced them. But, both heroes and statesman amid the din of arms, and the hurry of business, are often necessitated to invert the natural order of things; to fight before they are deliberate, and to decide before they consult. A statesman may regulate himself by events. But it is seldom that he can cause events to regulate themselves by him. It often happens, too, both in courts and in cabinets, that there are two things going on together, a main-plot, and an under-plot; and he that understands only *one* of them, will, in all probability, be the dupe of *both*. A mistress may rule a monarch, but some obscure favourite may rule the mistress.

Doctor Busby was asked how he contrived to keep all his preferments, and the head mastership of Westminster School, through the successive, but turbulent reigns of Charles the First, Oliver Cromwell, Charles the Second and James; he replied, "The fathers govern the nation; the mothers govern the fathers, but the boys govern the mothers, *and I govern the boys.*"

Thick Skull; advantages of having one

That which we acquire with the most difficulty, we retain the longest, as those who have earned a fortune, are usually more careful of it than those who have inherited one. It is recorded of Professor Porson that he spoke Greek fluently, when he could no longer speak English.

The professor was remarkable for a strong memory, which was not as puzzling as the great perfection of his other faculties; for, to the utter confusion of all craniologists, on examination after death, it turned out that this great scholar was gifted with the thickest skull of any professor in Europe. Professor Gall, on being called upon to explain this phenomenon, and to reconcile so tenacious memory, with so thick a receptacle for it, is said to have replied, "How the ideas got into such a skull is their business, not mine. I have nothing to do with that; but let them once get in — that is all I want; once in, I will defy them ever to get out again."

Time and Space; without limits
Time is the most indefinable, yet paradoxical of things; the past is gone, the future is not come, and the present becomes the past, even while we attempt to define it, and like the flash of the lightning, at once exists and expires — Time is the measurer of all things, but is itself immeasurable, and the grand discloser, but is itself undisclosed. Like space, it is incomprehensible, because it has no limit, and it would be still more so if it had.

If we stand in the middle of a dark vista, but with a luminous object at one end of it, and none at the other, the former will appear to be short, and the latter long. And so perhaps it is with time; if we look back upon time that is past, we naturally fix our attention upon some event with the circumstances of which we are acquainted, because they have happened, and this is that luminous object which apparently shortens one end of the vista, but if we look forward into time that is to come, we have no luminous object on which to fix our attention, but all is uncertainly, conjecture and darkness. As to time without an end, and space without a limit, these are two things that finite beings cannot clearly comprehend. But if we examine more minutely into the operations of our own minds, we shall find that there are two things much *more incomprehensible,* and these are time that *has* an end, and space that *has* a limit. For whatever limits these two things, must of itself be unlimited, and I am at a loss to conceive where it can exist, but in space and in time. But this involves a contradiction, for that which limits, cannot be contained in that which is limited.

We know that in the awful name of Jehovah, the Hebrews combined the past, the present, and the future, and St. John is obliged to make use of a periphrasis, by the expression, *who is, and was, and is to come.* Sir Isaac Newton considers infinity of space on the one hand, and eternity of duration on the other, to be the grand sensorium of the Deity. It is indeed a sphere that alone is worthy of Him who directs all the movements of nature, and who is determined by his own unalterable perfections, eventually to produce the highest happiness, by the best means ...

Tipping; running the gauntlet
Another of the minor miseries formerly imposed on society by the despotism of fashion, was the necessity of giving large sums, denominated "vails" to a whole bevy of butlers, footmen, and lacqueys. This was carried to such an excess, that no poor man could afford to dine with a rich one, unless he enclosed a guinea with his card of invitation; and yet this custom, more mean, if possible, than absurd, kept its ground until a few such men as Swift, Steele, and Arbuthnot, happened to make a discovery in terrestrial bodies, productive of more comfort than any made before or since, in those that are celestial.

After a due course of experiments, both synthetically and analytically pursued, they found out and promulgated to the world, that two or three friends, a joint of Welsh mutton, a blazing hearth, a bottle of old wine, and a hearty welcome at home, were far better things than cold fricassees, colder formalities, sour liquors, and sourer looks abroad, saddled moreover, with the penalty of running the gauntlet of a whole gang of belaced and betassled mendicants, who proceeded from the plunder of the pocket of the guest, to their still more barefaced depredations on the cellar of their master.

Torture; arguments against its use
The advocate for torture would wish to see the strongest hand joined to the basest heart, and the weakest head. Engendered in intellectual, and carried on in *artificial* darkness, torture is a trial not of guilt, but of nerve, not of innocence, but of endurance; it perverts the whole order of things, for it compels the weak to affirm that which is false, and determines the strong to deny that which is true; it converts the criminal into the evidence, the judge into the executioner, and makes a direr punishment than would *follow* guilt, *precede* it.

When under the cloak of religion, and the garb of an ecclesiastic, torture is made an instrument of accomplishing the foulest schemes of worldly ambition, it then becomes an atrocity that can be described or imagined, only where it has been seen and felt. It is consolatory to the best sympathies of our nature, that the hydra-head of this monster has been broken, and a triumph over her, as bright as it is bloodless obtained, in that very country whose aggravated wrongs had well nigh made vengeance a virtue and clemency a crime.

Universe, the; primary rules, ultimate goals
The farther we advance in knowledge, the more simplicity shall we discover in those primary rules that regulate all the apparently endless, complicated, and multiform operation of the Godhead. To Him, indeed, all time is but a moment, and all space but a point, and He fills both, but is bounded by neither. As merciful in his restrictions, as in his bounties, he sees, at one glance, the whole relations of things, and has prescribed unto himself one eternal and immutable principle of action; that of producing the highest ultimate happiness, by the best possible means. But he is as great in minuteness as in magnitude, since even the legs of a fly have been fitted up and furnished with all the powers, and all the properties of an air pump, and this has been done by the self-same hand that created the suns of other systems and placed them at so immense a distance from the earth, that light itself seems to lag on so immeasurable a journey, occupying many millions of years in arriving from those bodies unto us ...

And as the grand discordant harmony of the celestial bodies, may be explained by the simple principles of gravity and impulse, so also in that more wonderful and complicated microcosm, the heart of man, all the phenomena of morals are perhaps resolvable into one single principle — *the pursuit of apparent good;* for although customs universally vary, yet man, in all climates and countries is essentially the same ... It may be that we know less, but that less is of the highest value, first, from its being a condensation of all that is certain; secondly, from its being a rejection of all that is doubtful and such a treasure ... increases in value, even by its diminution.
For knowledge is twofold, and consists not only in an affirmation of what is true, but in the negation of that which is false. And it requires more magnanimity to give up what is wrong, than to maintain that which is right for our pride is wounded by the

114

one effort, but flattered by the other. But the highest knowledge can be nothing more than the shortest and clearest road to truth, all the rest is pretension, not performance, mere verbiage, and grandiloquence, from which we can learn nothing, but that it is the external sign of an internal deficiency.

But to revert to our former affirmation of the simplicity of those rules that regulate the universe, we might farther add, that any machine would be considered to be most ingenious, if it contained within itself principles for correcting its own imperfections. Now, a few simple but resistless laws have effected all this so fully for the world we live in, that it contains within itself the seeds of its own eternity. An Alexander could not add one atom unto it, nor a Napoleon take one away. A period, indeed, has been assigned to it by revelation; otherwise it would be far less difficult to conceive of its eternal continuance, than of its final cessation.

Unpopular Measures; how to get them passed
Shrewd and crafty politicians, when they wish to bring about an unpopular measure, must not go straight forward to work; if they do, they will certainly fail; and failures to men in power, are like defeats to a general, they shake their popularity. Therefore, since they cannot sail in the teeth of the wind, they must tack, and ultimately gain their object, by appearing at times to be departing from it. Mr. Pitt, at a moment when the greatest jealousy existed in the country, on the subject of freedom of the press, inflicted a mortal blow on this guardian of our liberties, without seeming to touch, or even to aim at it; he doubled the tax upon *all* advertisements, and this single act immediately knocked up all the host of pamphleteers, who formed the sharp-shooters and tiralleurs* of literature, and whose fire struck more terror into administration than the heaviest cannonade from bulky quartos or folios could produce; the former were ready for the moment, but before the latter could be loaded and brought to bear, the object was either changed or removed, and had ceased to awaken the jealousies or to excite the fears of the nation.
* skirmishers

Vanity; often leads to disappointments
Our vanity often inclines us to impute not only our successes, but even our disappointments, to causes personal, and strictly confined to ourselves, when nevertheless the effect may have been removed from the supposed cause, far as the poles asunder. A zealous, and in his way a very eminent preacher, whose eloquence is as copious and far more lucid than the waters of his beloved Cam, happened to miss a constant auditor from his congregation. Schism had already made some depredations on the fold, which was not so large, but to a practiced eye, the deduction of even one was perceptible.

What keeps our friend Farmer B. away from us? Was the anxious question proposed by our vigilant minister to his clerk? I have not seen him amongst us, continued he these three weeks. I hope it is not Socinianism that keeps him away. "No, your honour," replied the clerk, "it is something worse than that." "Worse than Socinianism! God forbid it should be Deism." "No, your, honour it is something worse than that."

"Worse than Deism! Good heavens, I trust it is not Atheism!" "No, your honour, it is something worse than that." "Worse than Atheism! Impossible; nothing can be worse than Atheism!" "Yes, it is, your honour — it is *Rheumatism!*"

Vox Populi, Vox Dei; some of the time
"*Vox Populi, Vox Dei*" "The voice of the people is the voice of God; this axiom has manifold exceptions and "*Populus vult decipi*"* is sometimes much nearer the truth; and Horace was of the same opinion, when he extolled that inflexible integrity which was not to be influenced by the "*Civium ardor prava jubentium*". ** The fury of the citizens insisting on that which was wrong. But this voice of the people has not only been violent where it was wrong, but weak and inefficient where it was right for the million though they are sometimes as strong as Sampson, are also as blind.

It happens that most of these great events which have been pregnant with consequences of the highest import to after times, have been carried, not with the voice of the people, but *against it*; they have been carried by active and enlightened minorities, having the means, in open contradiction to the will and the wishes of the majority. These political and moral whirlwinds, eventually productive of good, have proceeded in direct opposition to the breath of public opinion, as thunder-clouds against the wind.

But to show the truth of the position stated above, that popular opinion has been weak and inefficient, even when it was right, I might without danger of being contradicted, affirm that if heads could have been *fairly* counted, Socrates would not have been sacrificed in Athens, nor Charles in England, nor Louis in France. Rome would not have been deluged in blood by proscriptions at the instigation of a cruel triumvirate, who met to sacrifice friendship at the shrine of revenge. Nor would Paris have been disgraced by judicial murders, conducted by such a wretch as Robespierre, who had nothing brave about him, but the boldness with which he believed in the want of that quality in others.

These things are, if possible, more degrading to the people that permit them, than to the parties that perform them, and that era which was termed the reign of terror, has been more fitly designated as "*the reign of cowardice.*"
* "*the fury of the mob*"
** "*ever demanding what is wrong*"

Women; marriageable age in the East
Women in warm climates are marriageable, says Montesquieu, at eight or nine years of age; infancy and marriage, therefore, almost always go together, and women become old at twenty. Reason then, and beauty are never found together. When beauty wishes to sway, reason refuses it; and when reason might attain it, beauty is no more. And Prideaux, in his life of Mahomet, informs us, that Mahomet was betrothed to his wife Cadhisja, at five years old and took her to his bed at eight, and that in the hot countries of Arabia and the Indies, girls are marriageable at eight years old, and are brought to bed the year after.

Writers vs. Orators
Those talents that constitute a fine writer, are more distinct from those that constitute an orator, than might be at first supposed; I admit that they may sometimes be accidentally, but never necessarily combined. That the qualifications for writing and those for eloquence, are in many points distinct, would appear from the converse of the proposition, for there have been many fine speakers who have proved themselves bad writers. Abstractions of thought, seclusion from popular tumult, occasional retirement to the study, diffidence in our own opinions, deference to those of other men, a sensibility that feels everything, a humility that arrogates nothing, are necessary qualifications for a writer; but their very opposites would perhaps be preferred by an orator. He that has spent much of his time in a study will seldom be collected enough to think in a crowd, or confident enough to talk in one.

We may also add that mistakes of the pen in the study, may be committed without publicity, and rectified without humiliation. But mistakes of the tongue, committed in the senate, never escape with impunity *"Fugit irrevocable verbum."** Eloquence, to produce her full effect, should start from the head of the orator, as Pallas from the brain of Jove, completely armed and equipped. Diffidence, therefore, which is so able a Mentor to the writer, would prove a dangerous counsellor for the orator.

As writers, the most timid may boggle twenty times a day with their pen, and it is their own fault if it be known even to their valet; but, as orators, if they chance to boggle once with their tongue, the detection is as public as the delinquency; the punishment is irremissible, and immediately follows the offense …
* "the word uttered is irrevocable"

Charles Caleb Colton, His Life and Times

(Excerpts from an article published in *"The Gentlemen's Magazine"* in London in 1832.)

"Mr. Colton was educated at Eton and King's College, Cambridge, and probably related, how nearly, we know not, to Rev Barfoot Colton, who was elected from Eton to the same college in 1755, and afterwards, in 1788, became a Canon Residentiary of Salisbury. Mr. Caleb Colton was elected from Eton in 1796, and was after chosen Fellow of King's. He graduated B.A.1801, M.A. 1804. In 1801 he was presented by the college to the perpetual curacy of Iverton Prior's Quarter in Devonshire which may be held together with a Fellowship, and where he continued to reside for many years; we presume until presented by his college to the vicarage of Kew and Petersham in 1812."

*   *   *

"The eccentricities, and it may be added, irregularities, by which he was afterwards distinguished, were not entirely unknown there. On one occasion he was sent to read the "Visitation of the Sick" to a dying parishioner, who had amassed great wealth in the Indies. This visit occupied him till the instant when another clergyman had concluded the afternoon prayers in the great church at Tiverton. Colton rushed from the dying man's bedside into the pulpit, and for above an hour poured forth an extemporaneous flood of no ordinary eloquence in favour of strict morals, to the no small surprise of a numerous congregation, closing at length with 'You wonder to hear such things from me! But if you had been where I was just now, and heard and seen what I did, you would have been convinced it is high time to reform our courses and I, for my part, am determined to begin.' Alas, the next Sunday, he hurried over the reading of a fifteen-minute' discourse, and immediately after, the writer saw him placing his pointers in the basket behind, and his guns beside him in his gig and driving off toward a distant manor, to be ready for the next day's partridge-shooting."

*   *   *

A writer who gave an account of him (Colton), in a defunct periodical, 'The Literary Magazine', was introduced to Mr. Colton by an equally eccentric personage, the well-known Walking Stewart. 'The appearance of Mr. C. was,' he says, 'at once striking and peculiar. There was an indefinable something in the general character of his features, which, without being prepossessing, fixed the attention of a stranger in no ordinary degree. His keen grey eye was occasionally overshadowed by a scowl or inflexion of the brow, indicative rather of a habitual intensity of reflection than of any cynical severity of disposition. His nose was aquiline, or (to speak more correctly, if less elegantly) hooked; his cheek bones were high and protruding, and his forehead by no means remarkable either for its expansiveness, or phrenological beauty of development. There was a singular variability of expression around his mouth, and his chin was precisely what Laveter would have called an intellectual chin. Perhaps the shrewdness of his glance was indicative rather of extraordinary cunning, than of high mental intelligence."

*   *   *

"His usual costume was a frock coat, sometimes richly braided and a black velvet stock: in short, his general appearance was quite military; so much so, that he was often asked if he were not in the army. I am half inclined to believe that he courted this kind of misconception; as his reply was invariably the same; 'No, Sir, but I am an officer of the church *militant.*' Before they parted, Mr. Colton gave his new acquaintance a pressing invitation to breakfast next morning, and put a card into his hand, in which the name of the street and the number of the house were explicitly mentioned. The describer went and found — a marine-store shop! And thinking that after all there must be some mistake, he walked off. On again meeting Mr. Colton, the too fastidious stranger was reproached for his breach of appointment, and invited anew. 'The most exaggerated description of the garrets of the poets of fifty years ago,' says the visitor, 'would not libel Mr. Colton's apartment. Such of the panes as were entire were begrimed with dirt. As to the only two chairs in the room, while one, apparently the property of the poet, was easy and cushioned, and differing essentially in character from the rest of the furniture, the other one, a miserable rush-bottomed one, was awfully afflicted with the rickets. On the deal table at which the host was seated, stood a broken wine-glass half filled with ink, with a steel pen, which had seen some service, laid transversely on its edge which raised him to fame. Mr. Colton insisted that he should taste his wine, and going to the piece of furniture which contained his bed, opened a large drawer near the floor, which was filled with bottles of wine ranged in saw-dust, as in a bin. His hock and white hermitage were delicious, and the poet and auditor parted faster friends than ever."

*   *   *

"Toward the end of 1820 appeared "*Lacon,* or Many Things in Few Words", addressed to those who think", a thin, ill-printed seven-shilling octavo. It attracted much attention and praise. The name of Colton was thenceforth known to all, and when we find that the sixth edition of "*Lacon*" appeared in 1821, we need not wonder that "*Lacon,* Vol. II" appeared in 1822. The merits of this work are undeniable. It may be alleged, indeed, that the use of antithesis is too frequent, and that some of his ideas may be traced to "Bardon's Materials for Thinking" (a favourite work with Mr. Colton) others are taken from a work *supposed* to be known to all — "Bacon's Essays", but still, when all deductions are made, enough will remain to place the author of *Lacon* far above all his contemporaries in the art of making his readers 'think'."

*   *   *

"In 1822 Mr. C. re-published his 'Napoleon', with extensive additions, under the title of 'The Conflagration of Moscow'. The next that the public heard of him was at the time of the great sensation respecting Thurtell's murder of Weare. The Vicar of Kew had disappeared, he was known to be a regular gamester, and to have been frequently in the company of the murderer and the murdered. It was thought that he had fallen a victim to some of those he had selected for his habitual associates, but Thurtell denied this fact. Some time elapsed before it transpired, to the public at least, that Mr. Colton's disappearance had been voluntary, and that he had fled from his creditors, who struck a docket against him, and gazetted him as a wine-merchant.

*   *   *

"In November, 1827, on the latest day allowed by law, he appeared to take possession of his living; but in 1828 he finally lost it, by lapse, and the college appointed a successor. For the next two years, he was in America, travelling through the United States; from thence he transferred his residence to the Palais Royal, 'which is to Paris,' says Galignani's Guide, 'what Paris is to Europe, the centre of pleasure and vice!' He there expended considerable sums in forming a picture gallery, and every nook of his apartment was filled with valuable paintings. He then became known in the gaming *salons* of the Palais Royal and so successful was he that in a year or two he acquired the equivalent of 25,000 English pounds. But inveterate attachment to the gaming table again rendered him a beggar, and his excesses brought on a disease, to remove which a surgical operation became indispensable. The dread of this operation produced such an effect upon Mr. Colton's mind that he became almost insane, and finally blew out his brains, in order to avoid the pain of the operation."

*   *   *

"During his residence at Paris his mode of dress continued unchanged. He had only one room, kept no servant (unless a boy to take charge of his horse and cabriolet), he lighted his own fire, and performed all his other domestic offices himself. He printed at Paris, for private circulation, 'An Ode on the Death of Lord Byron' and continued to occupy himself in literary composition; and he has left a poem of 600 lines called 'Modern Antiquity' which will probably be published."

*   *   *

"Colton was in many respects a most singular character; but the distinguishing feature of his mind was promptitude. Well-read to intimacy, with the ancient classics, — after dinner, his Greek and Roman lore would flow as freely as his wine, affording a delicious feast to scholars. Nor was he less an admirer of what was excellent in morals. After hearing the present occupier of the late Robert Hall's pulpit in Cambridge, Colton introduced himself to spend the evening with the preacher; — then 'Greek met Greek' and brought out the stories of ancient literature and heathen and Christian ethics till after morning. 'We held a sober festival — that E----ds is a worthy fellow; sound in principle as erudite in learning'. It was erroneously stated, at the moment of Mr. Colton's death that he was in a state bordering on poverty: such was not the truth. He had been for a long time substantially assisted by his family, which is confirmed by a letter he wrote to his aged mother only a few days before the awful moment of his decease, in which he thanked her for her ample remittances."

A Preface to "Modern Antiquity" by Charles C. Colton which was published post-humously in 1835 by his friend of twenty years standing; Markham Sherwill.

"Mr. Colton (as I have already stated in a former page) was labouring under great pain from an old and inveterate complaint, at the time he finished the present poem. During the last four-and-twenty hours of his chequered life, he expressed to me more than once great doubt as to the probability of his recovery. I may say that he entertained a fear of death, and while apprehending that awful moment, a sudden aberration of mind called it to his relief. How strange that which he dreaded most, he courted as his only cure. We have witnessed moments when the best and most learned men resigned their powers of reflections into the hands of despair, and abandoned the idea that good even may be inculcated by an example of courage and resignation. The insufferable agony with which Mr. Colton was afflicted, seemed at once to dethrone his reason and render him the victim of derangement. Let us hope, in consideration of his respectable and extensive connections, that a pall will be drawn over those deviations which humanity is subject to. That the good which he may have done should not be evil spoken of, it is just that we should here state how invariably cautious he was of respect toward every hallowed subject, frequent in alleviating the miseries of others, even when in affliction himself, and lasting will be the benefits of his aphorisms to the studious and contemplative, and which, if carefully gleaned, must still the voices of the enemy and avenger, forcing even such to tread lightly over the ashes of his untimely grave."

**Hic Facet
Charles Caleb Colton
Requiescat In Pace**

"*MURMUR at nothing; if our ills are reparable, it is ungrateful, if remediable, it is vain. But a Christian builds his fortitude on a better foundation than Stoicism; he is pleased with everything that happens, because he knows it could not happen, unless it had first pleased God, and that which pleases him must be best. He is assured that no new thing can befall him and that he is in the hands of a Father who will prove him with no affliction that resignation cannot conquer or death cannot cure.*"